Creating a Safe Place

Creating
a Safe Place

Christians Healing from
the Hurt of
Dysfunctional Families

Curt Grayson and Jan Johnson

HarperSanFrancisco
A Division of HarperCollins*Publishers*

Library of Congress Cataloging-in-Publication Data

Johnson, Jan, 1952–
    Creating a safe place : Christians healing from the hurt of dysfunctional families / Curt Grayson and Jan Johnson. — 1st ed.
       p.   cm.
    Includes bibliographical references.
    ISBN 0-06-064306-4 (alk. paper)
    1. Adult children of dysfunctional families — Religious life.
    2. Twelve-step programs — Religious aspects — Christianity.
    I. Grayson, Curt. II. Title.
    BV4596.A274J64   1991
    248.8'6 — dc20   90-84439
                                              CIP

91 92 93 94 95 HAD 10 9 8 7 6 5 4 3 2 1

This edition is printed on acid-free paper that meets the American National Standards Institute Z39.48 Standard.

*To the New Hope Support Group at
First Evangelical Free Church, Fullerton, California,
and Free to Choose, Hope Chapel,
Hermosa Beach, California.*

We would like to thank:

Earl, whose words and silence helped create a
safe place, and my family, who, even through
the stormy times, let me know I was still loved.

—Curt

My husband Greg and my children Jeff and
Janae who are walking through my recovery
with me and who encouraged me while I walked,
talked, and dreamt this book.

—Jan

Contents

Creating a Safe Place

Introduction

What do you say to Christians who

- study the Bible and pray regularly but still fight bouts of depression that they can't explain?
- get mad at God when things go wrong?
- feel guilty because, even though they have "the answer" in Christ, "the answer" doesn't seem to work for them?

Both of us lived that dilemma for many years. We felt doubly guilty because, as a therapist (Curt) and a pastor's wife (Jan), we worked hard to help others but could not help ourselves. We had no idea that our problems were rooted in the ways we had responded to growing up in alcoholic homes.

As each of us went through personal crises, we were advised that we were adult children of alcoholics (ACAs) and that we should attend support groups. Both of us were privileged to attend churches that had support groups for adult children of dysfunctional families (ACDFs), and we reluctantly visited them. It took only one meeting to see that these meetings were safe places in which to find wholeness and to sort out our distorted views of God. We felt much like David of the Old Testament when he wrote,

> For in the day of trouble
>   he will keep me safe in his dwelling;
> he will hide me in the shelter of his tabernacle
>   and set me high upon a rock. (Psalm 27:5)

Much to our surprise, we found that the ACDF struggle is not uncommon in the church. We met many others with variations of our struggle, who lived in fear of being "found out" as less-than-adequate Christians. We have included some of their stories in this book. Many of them will probably sound familiar to you and will remind you of incidents from your own past. Expect feelings to come up that aren't pretty. Expect to learn how to face the pain of your past, to walk through it, and to grow.

We offer you ourselves in this book. We did more than research this material: we lived it. We attended secular Twelve-Step groups; we attended and led church-related Twelve-Step–style groups. In all these groups, we found safe places for ourselves.

Creating a Safe Place is also written for ACDFs who no longer attend church. Perhaps you lost interest in church, or you found that the church was no longer helping you get your spiritual needs met. We were both on the verge of joining those ranks when we began our ACDF recovery. We were burned-out Christians, tired churchgoers. We had misunderstood God and were worn out from trying to understanding him. We pray that if you feel this way, you will allow God to reignite your faith in him as you read this book.

As you examine your faith and work on your recovery, consider your role in creating safe places for other ACDFs. Perhaps you can use the tools in this book to start a support group and make it work. We believe that support groups can revitalize the church so that recovery experiences and spiritual growth can multiply.

Within this book, we want you to find hope and help. If you feel as if you don't fit in, or that your problems are beyond help, take heart as you read about our continuing journey—and we hope yours as well—as together we all find safe places to heal our hurts.

CHAPTER 1

"Saved," But Still Sick

Susan, Former Missionary,
Adult Child of an Alcoholic (ACA)

I accepted Christ just in time—the night before I had planned how I would commit suicide. My death would have shocked a lot of people. I had received my high school's "Most Likely to Succeed" award, and I'd been a homecoming queen nominee. No one knew that the reason I had backed out was that I was afraid I would lose and let everyone down. Besides, I was sure that if people knew the real me—not just the fragile facade I maintained—they would know I didn't deserve to win.

Then I heard that if I accepted Christ, I would have love, joy, and peace. I'd wanted those things all my life! On top of that, I would receive eternal life. But a few months after my conversion, the old feelings reared their heads. I felt empty and alone once again.

I was afraid, and I began to doubt my conversion. I "got saved" over and over—in hopes of rekindling those earlier excited feelings that now seemed out of reach.

I wondered if God was disappointed in me, or if I had angered him. I decided I wasn't good enough to be his child. From my experiences in an alcoholic home, I knew how to make people love me. I would be good, work hard, and help anyone I could.

Caretaking had always filled the emptiness inside me. When my mother divorced my alcoholic father and threw him out of the house, I visited him every day at his apartment. Many times he didn't have food, so I sneaked food out of our house to him.

As I thought about careers, I gravitated toward those that would allow me to take care of others. I decided to become a missionary. I was sure God would be pleased with this sacrifice, and he would love me for it.

Again, the emptiness was filled.

I worked in an orphanage in Kenya. But whenever I saw a lonely and hurting child, I would see myself and feel overwhelmed. My well-meaning Christian friends gave me the answer, "Pray harder, read the Bible more, and trust God to meet all your needs." I did this diligently, but it didn't seem to work. I didn't tell my friends, though, because they would think I wasn't spiritual.

Once, when I had dysentery, they prayed for me to be healed. I wasn't healed, and I was sure it was because I didn't have enough faith. I didn't want my friends to find this out.

I kept trying to reach more people. Even though we traveled from one tribe to another, it wasn't enough. I felt I was responsible for reaching every person on earth. I had to get up earlier, and I had to preach longer. I had to devise new methods.

When I taught Bible studies to refugees, they looked up to me and thought I was a good teacher. I felt so inadequate that I hated teaching. People were praising God, but I wanted to get away from it all. I thought I would never have the faith that others did.

I decided that the answer was to move to a more difficult country. So I signed up to work in a Hindu nation where anyone who was caught trying to convert someone received a seven-year prison sentence. Being a martyr had a double appeal for me: I could make God proud of me, and I could also die, which would relieve my emotional pain.

After three years, an illness forced me to return to the States. I became as depressed as I had been before accepting Christ. I talked to a Christian counselor, who immediately asked if I were from an alcoholic home. I was surprised that he thought this was connected to my depression. I had always thought my background was an advantage. Three of the other missionaries who had grown up in alcoholic homes agreed. We decided that our backgrounds had prepared us for a low level of living—we could live in mud huts and eat strange food and use a latrine. We believed also that we were stronger and more compassionate. Unlike other people, we could easily adapt because we had grown up never knowing what would happen next. Could my "great advantage" have been a problem all along?

My first visit to an ACA (adult child of an alcoholic) support-group meeting at a nearby church shocked me. All those normal-looking, "together"-type people felt as bad as I did inside. I began to weep and could not stop. I cried through the next six meetings, but mostly for joy. I was thrilled to find out that I wasn't crazy.

It was even more thrilling that these people were Christians who loved God as I did. I didn't have to pretend to be super-Christian anymore. I didn't have to manipulate them into loving me. I could be exactly who I was and still be loved.

*

Donna, Church Secretary, Adult Child of an Alcoholic Grandparent

"Is one of your parents an alcoholic?" my boss asked me.

I was angry. How could he, even though he was a minister, insinuate that my dad, my mom, or anyone else in my family could be an alcoholic? All I had done was ask his advice about a problem with my teenage son.

"Why do you ask?" I replied, keeping my usual calm church-secretary facade intact.

"Because so many feelings you describe fit the ACA profile."

I dismissed him with a polite smile, but I was still seething. I had typed those ACA characteristics many times for our church's ACA support-group brochures. Didn't I know something about this stuff?

A list of characteristics set on my desk even then, but I put it aside. As the day wore on, I began to remember my dad talking about how Grandpa used to be an alcoholic.

Later, by the copy machine, I quizzed my pastor/boss/friend: "Would it affect me if my grandfather were an alcoholic?" He said that it could, depending on how my father had reacted to his upbringing.

I sat at my desk and reread those ACA characteristics. Immediately, seven of them jumped off the page. This was me.

But it wasn't the "me" that my church friends knew. They knew an efficient good-deed-doer who whizzed through projects, who never made typing errors, and who always stayed late to finish her work. They would never guess that I was still so keyed up when I got home that anything my husband or son said would set me off.

I often took my husband's simple question "Are there any clean shirts?" as an attack on my selfhood. Many times he did the laundry himself to keep from stirring me up.

But I was never pacified. I continually got angry with my husband and son, and I felt discouraged about it. It seemed that no matter how hard I tried, happiness and contentment were only temporary.

That day in the office, I began to wonder if my dad, who was himself an ACA, had these feelings. He had been an only child, abandoned in his infancy by his mother. He was raised by his stern grandmother and his alcoholic father.

Dad could be warm, kind, and caring much of the time, but he was quick to explode, no matter who was around. He could be talking gently to me, handing me a glass of iced tea, when Mom might ask, "Why didn't you fix me a glass of tea?" Then he would explode. I felt embarrassed when he did that. I was always scared and unsure of what would happen next with him.

Mom also had been an only child. She had been raised by loving, but strict, legalistic parents. She had had to tow the line at all times, and she later treated my brother and me the same way. I learned early that if I talked back, I would get slapped or have my mouth washed out with soap. I learned that it was not okay to express real feelings—only what was acceptable to others.

So, as a child, I vented my anger by having fistfights with my brother. As an adult, I aimed all this anger at my husband and son. I acted just like my father—swearing, slamming doors, spitting out sarcastic put-downs. It was so ironic: I had promised God that I would never treat my son the way my parents had treated me, but I did it anyway. I never let my son act like a little boy. I disciplined him unfairly and made unreasonable demands on him; that was the only way I knew how to be a parent.

After that day at work, I attended our church's ACA support group. After the first meeting, I told my husband, "These people are a bunch of whiners," but by the next Tuesday I wanted to go back. I saw that these people weren't whiners at all—just more open than anyone I had ever met at church. That honesty and acceptance drew me until I was one of them, sharing my true self. I also decided to go to therapy.

I've since discovered more appropriate, healthy ways to express my anger. I've learned not to be so controlling of people. The other day, my twenty-two-year-old son asked my advice for the first time, because he knows that now that I'm in recovery, he'll get a simple opinion instead of a lecture.

For three years I lied to my parents about where I went on Tuesday nights. I was sure they wouldn't like it, so I told them I was going to a Bible study. Then a year ago, I spoke up.

My mom was complaining about Dad's angry outburst. "Have you ever told Dad how you feel about his behavior?" I asked.

"No. He wouldn't like that," she said, surprised.

I pushed on. "If you start telling him when he makes you feel uncomfortable, he might stop. Tell him you're not going to put up with that anymore."

My mother only stared.

"I know this, Mom, because I've been going to the ACA group at church. The way Dad acts when he's upset is inappropriate. He acts like an alcoholic."

My mom was offended and didn't respond. Yet she has brought it up now and then over the last year. I've left the door open.

I also talked to Dad that day. I was surprised that he was so vulnerable. He started talking about his childhood. I kept listening and asking questions. We talked so long that we missed our dinner reservations.

I have compassion for my mom and dad now. They grew up in dysfunctional families, too, and did the best that they knew how to do.

I left my position as church secretary. This was not a financially advantageous move, but my husband agreed that I needed time to get to know myself. Now that I've shed my "outstanding Christian" role, I enjoy going to church. I continue to emerge as a new person, which is exciting to me.

*

Matt, "Missionary Kid," Adult Child of a Dysfunctional Family (ACDF)

"Maybe you should come with me to an ACA meeting," my sister Marcia offered.

We had just finished a heavy talk about how I was more than normally afraid to ask girls out. I knew Marcia thought that going to the ACA group would help me, but our parents weren't alcoholics. It was silly to go there.

Yet I definitely had problems. First, there was my career. I had worked with several Christian advertising companies, but I had never stuck with anything. I lacked confidence, and I had no goals. At the age of thirty-one, I was in career transition, working as a clerk at a grocery store and attending school at night.

But worse, I was afraid to get close to people. I didn't initiate friendships easily, especially with women. Deep down, I suspected it had something to do with my upbringing. It had taught me early that if you get close to people, they go away or send you away.

When I was a child, my parents were missionaries in Pakistan, and I was sent to boarding school. I remember being six years old and feeling confused about why I couldn't live at home anymore. I felt abandoned and lonely, even though my older sister was nearby.

Boarding school is also where my problems with self-esteem began. After a happy year of living with my family on furlough, I returned to school to begin fourth grade. My teacher mistook my sadness for laziness and sent me to the principal's office many times. I often stayed after class to write punishment sentences five hundred times. At the end of the year, my teacher recommended that I repeat the fourth grade.

My parents decided to trust her judgment. To me, this validated my suspicion that I was not a smart person.

The next year, I had a different teacher, and my grades improved dramatically. But the other boys in my class didn't know that, and they called me "dummy" and asked me why my parents had kept me back. One boy, who had also done poorly but had not been held back, was especially merciless. Whenever I beat him in tetherball, he said, "You can't talk to me because you're dumb."

Throughout school, I was a year behind my original class, and I never forgot it. Even though my mother often apologized for following the teacher's advice, I still thought it was my fault.

Vacations were strained, too. My mother wanted to be perceived as a responsible missionary, who did her job efficiently and correctly. She was especially paranoid about being late, because it made a bad impression. I felt tense whenever our family went somewhere together.

I guess you would call my mother a perfectionist. She did all the missionary secretary work well. She kept the house fastidiously clean. I don't know if it's true, but I always felt that all the small things she worried about were more important than her children's feelings.

As the years passed, I distanced myself from my parents. It was too painful to leave them every year in the fall to go back to boarding school, so I made sure I never got close to them.

Coming back to the States for college didn't solve my problems, either. I continued to keep people at a distance. Small-group interaction threatened me. I didn't go to Bible studies unless I knew everyone well and trusted them.

When my parents announced that they planned to return to the States for good, Marcia urged me to go to counseling with her to prepare myself. There I began to discover why my life was so hollow.

When my parents arrived, Marcia and her husband confronted them. She let go of her pent-up anger and pain. I remember feeling protective of my parents and wanting Marcia to let them off the hook. Yet I knew that what she was saying was true. I felt the same abandonment and aimlessness that she felt.

My mother kept saying, "I can't change. I'm who I am. Don't talk to me about this." She and my father felt leery of psychologists and warned us against them.

It was at this point that I took Marcia's advice. I decided to try the support group for ACAs at my church. I immediately identified with the list of ACA characteristics so well. I listened to the people talk, and their stories sounded like mine. I knew at once I belonged there.

A few months later, I talked to my parents about how my childhood loneliness and fear were affecting me as an adult. At first, I calmly expressed my fears, but finally I began crying, releasing the anxiety of my childhood years to them. They listened quietly.

I love my parents and want to be close to them. I understand that they have hurts of their own, especially since their parents were divorced when they were young. My mom has even blurted out her own feelings of abandonment because her mother had left her with an aunt when she was only six years old. It seems like both my parents use workaholism to cover up these hurts.

I believe there is hope for healing my past. I'm learning to deal with my feelings of abandonment and insecurity. I look forward to establishing better relationships with others, and especially with God. I want to be the healthy person God intended for me to be.

*

Susan, Donna, and Matt are not misfits within the church. They are three of many Christians who are also adult children of dysfunctional families (ACDFs).

The ACDF label has grown out of the adult-children-of-alcoholics (ACA or ACoA) movement. This movement began when many of us who are grown children of alcoholics discovered that, even if we didn't drink, we were much like our parents. We felt depressed, and some of us frequently blew up in anger. We took care of others, as if the whole world were our parents, who needed us. We "numbed out" when strong feelings overwhelmed us, and we didn't open ourselves up to other people.

We wanted to change. Enough ACAs went to therapy that these therapists recognized a pattern: you could take the child out of the alcoholic family (when he or she left home), but you couldn't take that alcoholic family influence out of the child (even as an adult). The literature and self-help structure for ACAs developed and multiplied.

Then, adults who hadn't grown up in alcoholic homes began identifying with the ACA literature and going to support-group meetings. They experienced the same problems in their lives that ACAs did. Now, the broader term *adult children of dysfunctional families* is used to describe both ACAs and ACDFs with a dysfunctionality other than parental alcoholism.

We've discovered that ACDFs from nonalcoholic homes struggle as much or more than traditional ACAs. Their families didn't have an easily recognizable problem such as alcoholism, so their problems don't seem as real to others or even to themselves. It is easier for them to deny their problems and pretend that they are coping as adults.

What exactly is a dysfunctional family? It is one in which there are unhealthy relationship patterns between family members. For some reason, parents do not meet the emotional needs of their children.

Often, that reason is that one or both parents are compulsive in some way. These compulsions range from illegal- or prescription-drug use to an addiction to "too much of a good thing," such as work, church, or television. These parents may provide food, clothing, and shelter, but they don't know how to be emotionally available to their children.

Most experts agree that a majority of families in America are dysfunctional. Psychologist John Friel and counselor Linda Friel estimate that ninety to ninety-five percent of families are dysfunctional,[1] and family therapist Virginia Satir in her book *Peoplemaking* says that healthy families number about four in one hundred.[2]

No studies have been done, and they would be difficult to conduct, because dysfunctionality isn't easy to measure. There is some unhealthy parenting in the best families and some healthy parenting in the worst. Yet it is safe to say that many families are dysfunctional enough that when the children grow up, they don't know how to interact with others in healthy ways.

Christians who are ACDFs often feel like second-class believers. We find that our relationship with Christ has not freed us of the pain and guilt we learned as children, and we assume that that's our fault.

We are different from ACDFs without a background of faith, because we have spiritual issues that we need to sort out. All of a sudden, we have to be open about our feelings, and we're not sure that God approves of that openness. In fact, we reexamine many of our notions about God, including the distorted views of him that we learned indirectly from our upbringing.

ACDF recovery can be a time of developing a healthier, more honest faith. Our depleted inner resources make us painfully aware of our need for God, and we look to the church to provide a safe place to express the agony within us.

That can't happen until we investigate the roots of dysfunctional families and see that this is not a new problem. It's as old as Adam and Eve.

Section 1

The Problems
of Our Past

CHAPTER 2

Dysfunctionality:
The Handicap of Being Human

Perhaps you suspect that dysfunctionality is a newfangled psychological malady. Back in the "good old days," people were too busy planting crops and feeding chickens to worry about inner problems. Yet dysfunctionality flourishes even when no one talks about it, and it blooms wherever it's planted. The garden is the entire human race, and the growing season began with the fall of humanity.

Adam and Eve experienced regrets and dashed hopes just as many families do today. What could be more "downwardly mobile" than being banished from the Garden of Eden? The first couple may have seen themselves as "ineffective parents," especially when Cain, the first ACDF, killed his brother.

After the Fall, Adam and Eve found that they had a sin nature, and their relationships became unhealthy. Thorns and thistles grew not only from the ground, but between the two of them. Part of the curse was that they would try to control each other: "Your desire will be for your husband, and he will rule over you" (Gen. 3:16).

We can only guess how their self-esteem must have plummeted. The curse produced turmoil in the areas that give most of us a sense of value—making a living (tilling the fields) and childbearing (Gen. 3:16–19).

Even as the Fall occurred, Adam and Eve displayed the basic elements of dysfunctional family pain: denial, blame, isolation, and angry actions.

Denial ". . . they hid from the Lord God. . . ."

Being "in denial" means acting as if painful events have never occurred and as if painful feelings have never surfaced. Those in denial repress feelings in a desperate effort to forget pain. It rarely works for long.

Adam and Eve operated by the dysfunctional family's three rules of denial:[1]

Don't talk. Adam and Eve hid after they had disobeyed God by eating from the tree of the knowledge of good and evil (Gen. 3:8). They didn't seek God out in a healthy way, saying, "Look what we've done. Can we work this out?" When God confronted them, they didn't ask for forgiveness. They didn't talk things out or admit guilt.

Don't trust. Adam and Eve didn't check with God about the serpent's accusation. They seemed to accept the serpent's word as if God's word meant little (Gen. 3:4–6).

Don't feel. Even though Adam and Eve probably felt great sorrow, it is never expressed in the words of this passage. The only feeling acknowledged was when Adam said he was afraid: " 'I heard you in the garden, and I was afraid because I was naked; so I hid' " (Gen. 3:10). Even this sounds more like a defense than like an admission of feeling.

Adam and Eve then busied themselves with a "solution"—sewing together fig-leaf garments, which God eventually replaced (Gen. 3:7, 21). In the same way, we often busy ourselves when we should be admitting feelings (although we don't know that Adam and Eve sewed leaves for this specific purpose).

Denial involves hiding, and dysfunctional families hide the truth about themselves. Even though the tension was thick in our own dysfunctional homes, we wanted others to think that we were from happy families. Even as adults, we hide our faults just as Adam and Eve did when they wouldn't admit their part in the "tree of knowledge" fiasco. We deny that our upbringing affected us. Like Susan, we may even say that we are better and stronger because of it.

Denial has three faces: the good, the bad, and the ugly.

The good. Denial seemed to work when we were children. We simply blocked out the painful experiences. Those who experienced physical and sexual abuse even managed to temporarily "forget" about it. In reality, we stored all these experiences in our subconscious minds, which became holding tanks for our pain.

Our dysfunctional families wanted so much to be healthy that they pretended they were. Our parents denied that anything was wrong, and since we wanted to please our parents, we pretended, too.

Those of us who were good at pretending shut out the family pain and anger and put on a "looking-good kid" image. When we made our parents happy, they told us, "You're looking good!" These compliments helped us bury the pain under our happy, self-confident facades of smiles.

Yet this "looking-good kid" image didn't help the problem; it only hid and delayed the problem. Perhaps God in his mercy allowed this delay so that as adults we could face the traumas we weren't equipped to deal with as children.

The bad. As adults, we continue to block out painful experiences, and we store them in the holding tanks of our subconscious minds. We don't know how to deal with life, so we don't deal with it at all. As we ignore our feelings, our relationships suffer. We do hurtful things that we don't understand, and we get stuck in patterns that confuse us. Nothing seems to work for us, but we don't know why.

The ugly. The holding tanks of our subconscious minds get so full of painful experiences that they explode. We find ourselves faced with divorces and unhappy children. If we were ever fortunate enough to choose a career and pursue it, we sabotage it. We find ourselves embroiled in problems such as alcoholism and compulsive overeating, allergies and psychosomatic illnesses, stress disorders and "frozen rage."

This explosion isn't all that bad. It forces us out of denial, and it becomes the gateway to getting the emotional garbage out of our lives. It doesn't feel good, but it's good for us.

Denial is what fuels dysfunctionality. Healthy people avoid denial because they admit their mistakes, find forgiveness, and go on. As children in dysfunctional families, we used denial to cope; now, as adults, we routinely deny our hurt and anger.

Understanding our own denial is difficult because we live in degrees of awareness. Some of us know that we have personality problems, but we refuse to deal with them. Others of us are not as aware. Problems seem to fade and then return. An insight or memory from the past may crystallize subtly, but we choose not to face it, so it hides itself again.

At times, well-meaning Christians may encourage denial by asking, "Isn't this 'dysfunctional family' business part of the past that you should put behind you?" We have a difficult time explaining that we *tried* putting it behind us; actually, we put it in our holding tanks, which exploded all over us.

Blame "It was her fault, God."

Adam blamed his sin on Eve. Eve blamed the serpent, and the first "blame loop" formed (Gen. 3:12, 13). Both

Adam and Eve tried to look good in God's eyes—as if they could manipulate God's opinion.

We blame others so that we can shift the responsibility for our actions away from ourselves.

- "I wouldn't be this way, except. . . ."
- "If you hadn't said that to me, then. . . ."
- "I can't help the way I am because. . . ."

The blame loop works both ways, creating two opposite effects in ACDFs. We blame others for our problems, or we reverse the flow and judge ourselves without mercy. *Maybe it's my fault,* we think, even when logic disproves it.

Blame becomes a way of life. In a crisis, it never occurs to us to look for solutions; we look for someone to blame.

Isolation ". . . I was afraid because I was naked; so I hid."

When Adam and Eve heard God walking in the garden, they hid, instead of walking with him (Gen. 3:8–10). They isolated themselves from God, rather than seeking comfort from God, who was the most able to give it.

As ACDFs, we condemn ourselves to solitary confinement. To keep up that "looking-good kid" image, we can't let anyone get close to us. We refuse to share our real selves, because others might find out how broken we are inside. This self-inflicted isolation depresses us.

We isolate ourselves because we learned to be comfortable with isolation as children in our dysfunctional families. Our parents—perhaps unintentionally—abandoned us emotionally by not expressing themselves in open and honest ways. Now, as adults, we feel that others hold back or reject us, even when they don't.

At times, honest, genuine contact with others entices us, but we know it's too dangerous to risk it. When as children we shared our feelings honestly in our unhealthy families, we got hurt. Our feelings weren't accepted or validated, so now we keep them to ourselves. We're so used to doing this that reaching out to others is a foreign, painful experience.

When people are bold enough to be real with us, it scares us, and we abandon them. Or we sabotage these "real" friendships by mistreating these friends so that they *will* abandon us.

Angry Actions "So Cain was very angry, and his face was downcast."

Cain became angry that his sacrifice wasn't as acceptable as that of his brother Abel. God acknowledged Cain's normal feelings of anger but urged him to "do what is right" (Gen. 4:6, 7). Instead of doing the right thing by preparing another sacrifice, Cain killed his brother (Gen. 4:1–8). He chose to act on his anger.

Rejection or failure devastates ACDFs just as it did Cain. We don't roll with the punches. Other people's victories threaten us and tell us that we will never be good enough.

Our anger erupts in inappropriate outbursts. We explode, and, like Cain, we may even lie to cover it up. When God asked Cain where Abel was, Cain lied. " 'I don't know,' he replied. 'Am I my brother's keeper?' " (Gen. 4:9).

We learned denial, blame, isolation, and angry actions in our homes, and now these attitudes handicap our growth. Intimate relationships are difficult because they require openness and authenticity, and we don't know how to act that way. We blame our spouses, parents, and employers for our problems, alienating them further. We don't risk expressing ourselves because it wasn't a safe thing to do as a child. We try to control those we love, and we project the anger of our childhoods on them. We look at friends from healthier homes and wonder how they can cope as well as they do.

Dysfunctionality or Sin?

Some people may look at these destructive tendencies and think that dysfunctionality is simply a fancy name for sin. Dysfunctionality is not sin; it's a by-product of sin. It's the handicap of an inability to relate to God and others because we were nurtured improperly as children.

David Seamands calls this a "chain reaction" and describes it in his book *Healing for Damaged Emotions:* "Beginning with the first sin of Adam and Eve, there was set in motion a chain reaction of imperfect parenting, through failures and ignorance and misguided actions, and worst of all, through conditional love."[2]

This imperfect parenting takes many forms. Without realizing it, our parents may have misrepresented God as a shaming and manipulating parent. They may have been so busy with their dysfunctionality that they violated our fragile childhood self-esteem by not giving us the love and attention we needed. So, as adults, we have a skewed view of God, and we lack necessary relationship skills.

You have no doubt heard the saying, "As the twig is bent, so goes the tree." Dysfunctionality is the bending of that twig. The twig continued to grow incorrectly because it didn't get what it needed. As a full-grown tree, the bent twig does the best it can, which is often sinful behavior growing out of two sources: dysfunctional family experiences and the sin nature.

Our sin nature seems to take dysfunctionality and run with it. We blame, we get angry, we turn to addictions. Even if we love God, we find the sin nature bullying us around. The apostle Paul felt this keenly: "I know that nothing good lives in me, that is, in my sinful nature. For I have the desire to do what is good, but I cannot carry it out" (Rom. 7:18).

For example, Patrick grew up in a home where his parents often argued with each other and yelled at him. He resented his parents for this and vowed he would never yell at his own children. Now as a parent, Patrick battles the temptation to yell at his children daily. Dysfunctionality is the presence of this gnawing temptation in Patrick's life and the probability that he will give in to it because children—even adult children—tend to imitate parents. Sin is what happens if he does give in.

Dysfunctionality may be part of the punishment extended to children for the sins of the fathers to the third and fourth generation. Sin often hurts innocent bystanders, and in family dysfunctionality, the effects of parents' sin spill over to their children and grandchildren.

This spillage of sin doesn't at all mean that we are doomed. Deuteronomy 5:10 adds that God shows "love to a thousand generations of those who love me and keep my commandments."

Yet no matter how dysfunctional our parents may have been, there is hope as we learn to love God and follow his ways. Patrick doesn't have to yell at his children as his parents did. He can seek help for his tendency toward anger. He can open himself to God, who is the ultimate loving parent who can help us find wholeness.

Recovery: Defeating the Heat of the Curse

The process of overcoming the poor effects of our upbringing is called *recovery*. At its core, recovery is a spiritual activity. It is the process of becoming a whole person who relates to God as the caring person that God is. Recovery involves shedding the "acts of the sinful nature," which produce further dysfunctionality, and growing in the "fruit of the Spirit" (see Gal. 5:19–23).

Too often, recovery is defined by short-term goals, such as

- learning to deal with life's hurts
- overcoming compulsions
- curbing angry outbursts

Recovery involves the whole person: we grow spiritually, psychologically, emotionally, socially, and physiologically.

Recovery is a lifelong process. We continue to deal with painful memories, to battle our compulsive tendencies, to release our frozen rage throughout our lives. For the Christian, recovery becomes part of that never-ending path of spiritual growth. We never "arrive," because we stay willing to change our sinful tendencies and our distorted beliefs about God.

Recovery is similar to the way that handicapped persons who need wheelchairs adapt to society. They go to physical therapy so that they can get maximum use out of seemingly useless limbs. They use motor-powered wheelchairs to keep up with others. They work around their handicaps by taking the extra time needed to find ramps. They understand and appreciate the small successes.

In our recovery from dysfunctional upbringing, we learn what our particular handicaps are. We work on becoming as functional as possible. We use the tools we need (books, counseling, support groups) to keep up with the stresses of life. We allow ourselves time and space to work out our recovery—and we understand that God allows us the same.

You may be wondering . . .

Q *Are you saying that parents are to blame for ACDFs' problems?*

A No. We are all free to choose our own courses of action. The dysfunctional family does, however, set up ACDFs to face a great deal of temptation and despair, which often leads to compulsions and physical disorders.

As we examine how the dysfunctional family works, our purpose is not to shift blame onto our parents; it is to understand why we act the way we do so that we may experience recovery. Forgiving and accepting our parents, which we will discuss in Chapter 13, is an important part of recovery.

Besides, many parents were well meaning in their attempts to nurture us. Many of them made heroic attempts in spite of their own dysfunctional backgrounds and seemingly impossible marriages. Some of them partially worked through their handicaps and, as a result, passed on less dysfunctionality to us than they received from their parents. As a result, our own struggles may be less severe than theirs were.

CHAPTER 3

What It Was Like
To Be a Child in a
Dysfunctional Family
(Part 1)

The healthy version of childhood is that children feel safe and loved. Jesus demonstrated this kind of nurturing when he blessed the children (Mark 10:13–16). When the disciples tried to push the children away (as dysfunctional parents often do), Jesus demanded to see the children. He focused his full attention on them, he listened to them, he touched them. He let the disciples know that children are precious people worthy of his time.

Society, however, has figured that if children aren't being beaten, starved, or sexually abused, their families aren't dysfunctional. Now we are recognizing that emotional abuse or emotional abandonment can be damaging as well and that, because it is so much more subtle, it is easier to deny.

The following characteristics describe what happens to children as emotional abuse occurs. The descriptions explain why children may grow up to be ACDFs who don't talk, trust, or feel.

Characteristics of Dysfunctional Families

A King Baby parent. One parent rules the dysfunctional family as "King Baby," a popular Alcoholics Anonymous term used at Alcoholics Anonymous meetings for the alcoholic parent. Even in non-alcoholic families, King Baby parents rule their families and force their wishes on others, which makes them "kings."

King Baby parents also demand that their needs be met, which makes them the "babies." If they don't have access to what they are addicted to (even something as intangible as power or sympathy), they upset the entire family by trying to get it. Spouse and children alike put that parent's needs before their own. To a greater or lesser degree, King Baby parents dominate and victimize family members who will let them.

This King Baby role may have developed over several generations. Perhaps Grandma "got sick" when she didn't get her way. Or Grandpa had a traffic accident whenever things were tense in the family. In these subtle ways, they gained the attention of family members and maintained control over them. This controlling behavior intensified in the next generation as their children became workaholics or tyrant-parents.

Many King Baby parents are alcoholics, yet their children don't realize it. ACA expert and psychologist Dr. Claudia Black didn't realize her father was an alcoholic until she enrolled in a class on alcoholism as part of her training. Sure, he drank excessively on a daily basis, but she never thought about it. Black guesses that forty percent of those who have grown up in alcoholic homes don't realize that their mothers or fathers were alcoholics.[1]

Perhaps that's because many alcoholics display a respectable image. They don't remind us of the drunks lying in the street. Alcoholics are usually ACDFs themselves, and they know how to be "looking-good kids." Gretchen's story illustrates this:

> A few friends in college attended ACA meetings. When they told me their stories about drunken parents

crashing their birthday parties, I thanked God that my parents weren't alcoholics.

One time they mentioned that ACAs often create chaos wherever they go. They explained that ACAs don't mean to do this, but they're so used to chaos from their upbringing that they constantly stir things up. I thought about how true that was for me. I like to shock people, to make things seem worse than they are. If I'm getting along okay with a boyfriend, I start a fight just to get a little drama going. It's as if I'm an excitement junkie.

As they talked, I wanted to melt into my chair. Never had anyone diagnosed my problem so clearly. I felt as if a huge spotlight were shining on me. Could this be why I had so many relationship problems?

I made an excuse to leave. My mind raced. I was sure my dad wasn't an alcoholic. He drank beer, but he never drank hard liquor. He hung out in bars, but he was a brilliant man and had held several high-paying positions. Of course, he was fired from his last job for losing his temper too many times.

Later that day, I told my friends I would go to their ACA meeting "to support them." There I got hold of an AA pamphlet with the quiz from Johns Hopkins University that helps alcoholics identify themselves.*

I answered the twenty questions from my dad's point of view. "He" scored a "9," well beyond the count of those who "definitely have a problem with alcohol."

I remembered more about his drinking. I had rarely ever seen him drunk, but he talked about drinking all the time. We couldn't go anywhere that he didn't drink or get antsy for a drink. We used to carry beer in the trunk of our car all the time. I'm shocked to think that he could be an alcoholic—I thought that people dressed in business suits were okay.

---

*The quiz is titled "Are You an Alcoholic?" and is printed at the end of this chapter.

Alcoholism abounds. According to the National Association for Children of Alcoholics, one in three families reports alcohol abuse by a family member.[2] Alcoholism afflicts eighteen million people in the United States,[3] and an estimated twenty-eight million Americans are children of alcoholics, with seven million of them being under eighteen years of age.[4]

Alcoholism can affect several generations. The family of Donna, the church secretary profiled in the first chapter, illustrates this. Donna's father, the child of an alcoholic, didn't drink, but he adopted the alcoholic King Baby disposition of his father. Eventually, Donna adopted it, too.

King Baby parents who aren't alcoholic are usually addicted to something else. Often, it's legal prescription drugs—especially Librium℗, Valium℗, or other sedatives. Or they may be addicted to sex, stress, relationships, church, power or control, gambling, cigarettes, sugar, salt, caffeine, money, or television. Anything parents do compulsively that takes attention away from important issues of life will affect children.

In some families, a King Baby situation is created through divorce or sickness. Family life revolves around nurturing a lonely single parent or a parent who is chronically ill. The children don't get the nurturing they need but are expected to be the ones to do the nurturing.

The nonalcoholic dysfunctional family should be taken as seriously as the alcoholic family. For example, the New Hope Support Group at the Evangelical Free Church in Fullerton, California, was started for ACAs. Soon, adult children from other types of dysfunctional families wanted to attend as well.

Curt tells how he first heard about this need:

> Two or three years ago, a woman asked to speak to me privately. She seemed upset, so I took her aside, and we talked.

"I want you to know that, quite honestly, I shouldn't even be here," she started out hesitantly.

"Why not?" I asked.

She looked at the floor. "My parents aren't alcoholics, and my grandparents weren't alcoholics."

Then she paused, looked up, and gave me a hopeful smile as she said, "But I could check to see if maybe my great-grandparents were."

She was trying to convince me to let her stay in the support group even though she didn't have an alcoholic parent.

"I have the same problems these ACAs have," she went on. "I belong here. For the first time in my life, I feel like I belong."

Of those who now attend the New Hope Support Group, one-third or more do not have a recognizably alcoholic parent.

Codependent family members.   In a dysfunctional family, the spouse and children put up with, and even take care of, the King Baby parent. Their behavior is labeled *codependent* because they act, react, and even "feed" on King Baby's dependent (or compulsive) behavior. It makes them feel needed, and subconsciously they've gotten used to that, and they like it.

Susan, the former missionary in the first chapter, was codependent on her alcoholic father when she sneaked food out of her house to give to him. She knew he needed her, and without realizing it, she liked being important enough to be needed.

Here's how a codependent spouse typically feels:

> I love my husband, but I can't stand him. He keeps our family in an uproar, so it's my responsibility to calm everyone down. I pretend it doesn't bother me, and I help my children get over the upsets.

Before he gets home, we scurry to pick things up and make sure his green La-Z-Boy chair is in exactly the right spot and free of toys. Then we tiptoe around him after he arrives.

I try to protect my children by not letting them bring friends home. They'll be embarrassed if their dad and I fight or if he starts yelling at them to redo their chores.

Sometimes I wonder if his outbursts are my fault. If I were a better housekeeper or a better lover, his needs would be satisfied. Other times, I see that he's a wonderful man, and I'm glad I'm sticking it out. When he's happy, we're happy. When he's miserable, we're miserable.

Codependent spouses usually teach their children to be codependent as well. Soon the entire family focuses their attention on pleasing and protecting King Baby. Codependent spouses don't like being controlled this way, and they retaliate by trying to control others. "How can I get my husband to behave the way I want him to? If I could do that, my life would be okay."

To escape the tiresome routine of nurturing the King Baby parent, codependent spouses wrap themselves in their own compulsions. They "numb out," which causes them to be unfocused and not fully present for their child. When this happens, the child doesn't get the full attention of either parent.

One of the many sad features of codependency is that it *enables* King Baby. Susan enabled her father to keep drinking because she took care of his needs for food. Like many alcoholics, her father wouldn't become desperate enough to seek recovery until he had nowhere else to turn. In his case, he could always turn to Susan.

Poorly bonded parents. Dysfunctional parents don't encourage each other. Some spend little time together, and they fight when they do. Others peacefully coexist in a state of cold war. In both cases, the parents are emotionally divorced, if not legally divorced.

To compensate for the weak marital bond, they often use other people to meet their needs or to act as a buffer. The mother may lean on her own mother or her daughter instead of on her husband for companionship. If a husband needs his self-esteem built up, he may seek love and recognition from his daughter or his sister or his secretary, not his wife. Children who are used this way by parents feel inappropriately important because they fill in the gaps in the marital relationship. It divides the parents even more. Here is a typical example:

> Marcia wanted to plant a garden, but her husband Ralph wasn't excited about it. When Jeff, her teenage son, got home from school, she told him about how his father was being his typically uncooperative self. Could Jeff help her with the tomato plants she bought?
>
> Jeff stood there, weighing the decision. He looked at the basketball in his hands; he had planned to play ball with his friends. He could tell his mom needed him, though, and after all, she gave him money whenever he needed it. She defended him to his dad when he got into trouble. Jeff tossed away the basketball and went to help his mom.
>
> When Ralph got home, Marcia rubbed it in that Jeff "had to" help her. Ralph only rolled his eyes. Jeff felt ashamed because he was sure he was widening the gap between his parents. But then he and his dad were miles apart anyway—what did it matter if his dad didn't like it?

Jeff suffered at the hands of both parents. His father ignored him, and his mother leaned on him for support as she would a spouse. Jeff felt he owed his mother some attention, since she lived for him. Since neither parent focused on Jeff's needs, Jeff was, in a sense, raising himself.

These inappropriate roles set the stage for *triangulation,* which occurs when one family member uses another family member as a go-between. Perhaps your father told you things he wanted your mother to know and figured that you would tell her. This roundabout sort of communication becomes a habit among all the family members. Even when children become adults, it continues. Mom now tells you that your sister should get a better job. Your mother expects you to speak to your sister for her. Though triangulation is often done to avoid hurting someone's feelings, it creates misunderstandings and strangles communication. It overburdens innocent bystanders with information (usually negative) that they don't need to know.

Parents in relatively healthy families illustrate the slogan "The best thing a father can do for his children is love their mother." The parents communicate with each other directly, they try to meet each other's needs, and together they work at meeting their children's needs. Because parents support each other, they can be fully present for their children.

When these children grow up, they know something about the skills that they need to nourish a healthy marriage. They've seen their parents solve problems and laugh together. ACDFs, however, didn't see this as children, so when they get married they don't know how to act. If they're wise enough to try to act differently from their parents, they often end up imitating them anyway.

Inappropriate role models.   Parents in unhealthy families don't show their children what mature adults are supposed to be. These parents act childishly: they manipulate, they pout, they throw tantrums. Kids grow up thinking that this babyish behavior is appropriate in adults.

When mature behavior is needed in a dysfunctional household, it is often the children who display it. Role reversal is common. Kids comfort and soothe their parents.

At the age of ten, Tim began "rescuing" his mother.

> One time my mom was lying on our old green
> couch, crying, and she asked me, "Why shouldn't I kill
> myself?"
> I was only in fifth grade, and I didn't know what to
> say. I looked through the doorway into the kitchen. The
> oven door was open, and I thought of a reason that
> made sense to me: "You make great pizza, Mom. You
> put all that gooey cheese and stuff on it."
> To my surprise, she smiled. She lay there for a
> while, and then she got up and fixed dinner. *I've helped
> her!* I thought. I felt powerful that I could prevent my
> mother's suicide.
> As a young adult, I sensed that my role was to take
> care of people as I had done with my mother. I became
> a pastor, clueless that I was listening to the voice of my
> broken childhood telling me that I should take care of
> others. I just thought I wanted to help humanity.

Tim's false feelings of "rescuing" power also led to a
false sense of guilt:

> When my mother would get depressed, I would
> sometimes tease her and try to make her laugh. She
> would feel better for a while. Other times, she would still
> be down. Then I felt as if I had failed. I hadn't tried
> hard enough. I wasn't clever enough.
> Eventually, I felt as if her problems were my fault.
> Guilt permeated my life. Even when I became a Chris-
> tian as a teen, I felt guilty before God. I felt like I had to
> perform by leading, teaching, singing. I *had* to do it all,
> compulsively. I worried that my salvation was slipping.

In this way, Tim's childhood set the tone for his life. As
a therapist, he devoted his life to listening to people and
offering pat solutions. He felt guilty when his clients lan-
guished.

One result of role reversal is that children grow up too fast. They aren't allowed to be kids. Tim jokes, "I figure I started counseling twenty years before I was licensed, since I started giving my mother advice when I was seven." The upshot of this childhood counseling role is that he, like many "caretaker" ACDFs, felt burned out before he ever became an adult.

You may be wondering . . .

Q *What are the characteristics of the typical alcoholic?*
A Here is the questionnaire used by Johns Hopkins University:

Are You an Alcoholic?

	YES	NO
1. Do you lose time from work due to drinking?	___	___
2. Is drinking making your home life unhappy?	___	___
3. Do you drink because you are shy with other people?	___	___
4. Is drinking affecting your reputation?	___	___
5. Have you ever felt remorse for drinking?	___	___
6. Have you gotten into financial difficulties as a result of drinking?	___	___
7. Do you turn to lower companions and an inferior environment when drinking?	___	___
8. Does your drinking make you careless of your family's welfare?	___	___
9. Has your ambition decreased since drinking?	___	___
10. Do you crave a drink at a definite time daily?	___	___
11. Do you want a drink the next morning?	___	___
12. Does drinking cause you to have difficulty sleeping?	___	___
13. Has your efficiency decreased since drinking?	___	___
14. Is drinking jeopardizing your job?	___	___

15. Do you drink to escape from worries or trouble?   ___ ___

16. Do you drink alone?   ___ ___

17. Have you ever had a complete loss of memory as a result of drinking?   ___ ___

18. Has your physician ever treated you for drinking?   ___ ___

19. Do you drink to build up your self-confidence?   ___ ___

20. Have you ever been to a hospital or institution on account of drinking?   ___ ___

If you answer yes to any *one* of the questions, that is a definite warning that you may have a problem with alcohol. If you say yes to any *two*, chances are you have a problem. If you answer yes to *three* or more, you definitely have a problem with alcohol.

CHAPTER 4

What It Was Like
To Be a Child in a
Dysfunctional Family
(Part 2)

Many people muddle over whether their families were dysfunctional or not. Or they understand that most families have some dysfunctionality, so they compare their families with others. *If mine wasn't as bad as yours,* they reason, *I don't have to worry.* That can be a subtle form of denial.

The more helpful question is, In what ways was my family dysfunctional and how is that dysfunctionality affecting me now? Here are a few more characteristics of dysfunctional families to help you figure that out. See which ones apply to your childhood family, and ask yourself how that dysfunctionality influences you as an adult.

Inconsistent discipline and love. Children can break the same rules two days in a row and be spanked one day but ignored the next. What's good on Tuesday is bad on Wednesday. They never know how their parents will react, so they check the tension barometer immediately when they walk into their houses. Tony tells his experience:

> My mom was stressed out that day, but I didn't know it. Like most other nine-year-olds, I couldn't let a creamy pan of fudge harden on the counter without sampling some of it. So I swooped my finger down the side of the pan while my mom was looking into the refrigerator.
>
> She wheeled around and yelled, "Tony, how many times do I have to tell you not to do that?" Then she

grabbed my hair and slapped me across the face several times with a wooden spoon until it broke.

I stood there stunned. My cheeks stung, and my scalp throbbed. I fled to my room, feeling violated. I knew I didn't deserve such a harsh punishment.

An hour later, my dad came to me and said, "You need to understand that your mother is under a lot of stress. Don't be too hard on her. Try not to upset her."

Even as a child, I knew my mom was wrong for slapping me that way. I knew that my dad shouldn't have excused her behavior and put the responsibility on me to understand her and please her. My mom should have come in and apologized. Yet how could I complain? My dad and mom were the minister and his wife.

Sometimes my parents could be neat people, but I never knew what would set my mom off. On another day I might have swiped a finger full of fudge and she would laugh and rumple my hair. I never knew what was going to happen.

Some have said that the only thing about a dysfunctional family that's consistent is that it's inconsistent. The parents show their love based on how they feel that day. If they've been able to practice their compulsion, or if the children have made them proud, they show love to their children. If the parents are upset, or if the children have disobeyed, the parents are preoccupied or distant. The children feel insecure and unsure about what might happen.

Healthy parents, however, work at praising and reinforcing their children. The children know what consequences to expect for wrong behaviors and can count on their parents to be fair. These parents also express unconditional love. They accept their children's mistakes and communicate that they love their children no matter what.

Inappropriately expressed feelings. Parents in dysfunctional families often express their emotions in extremes.

They may relish in ecstasy over a neighbor child who simply brings them the newspaper, or they may blow up in anger over a broken tool.

The outbursts, especially, scare the entire family, including the King Baby parent. Family members eventually try to suppress normal emotions as well. Whenever the children risk expressing deep feelings, their words are either ignored or blatantly denied: "You shouldn't feel so unhappy. It's nothing."

Children need to express their feelings, especially feelings of fear. In dysfunctional families, the children seldom do so because they don't want someone either fawning over them or yelling at them. As a result, the children don't receive the comfort they need, and they escape into snacks, television, or even addictions. They often feel hopeless, thinking they'll never get their needs met. They illustrate the Bible verse "Hope deferred makes the heart sick" (Prov. 13:12). As they become adults (ACDFs), they often face despair and depression but don't know why.

Violated Boundaries.   Some parents invade their children's "space" and dominate their world. They build their lives around their children and become entangled in their children's relationships. As their children grow older, the parents can't let go of them.

When these children become adults, they find that they don't know how to be responsible and independent. Ruth Ann's parents have always controlled her life, but now she is trying to break away.

> I constantly tell my mother to leave me alone. She calls me at my apartment and gives me advice—get this job, buy this sofa, move closer to me. I hate it.
>
> What really bothers me, though, is that sometimes I ask for her advice. When I don't, I find myself thinking, *Now, what would Mom tell me to do?*

I rely on my parents too much. I was in a wreck last year, and my car was towed to a gas station. I didn't tell my parents, because I was trying to be independent. But I didn't call the insurance company, either. I couldn't figure out what to do. My parents had always done these things for me. Besides, they had given me the down payment for the car (and had chosen the exact car, of course). What would they say about the wreck?

Finally, they figured out that I was riding the bus all the time, and they quizzed me about my car. My dad called the insurance company and went to the gas station to check on my car. I hate to admit that I was relieved. It scares me to think that I subconsciously put off doing anything because I knew my parents would bail me out if I waited long enough.

Some parents violate their children's boundaries with sexual or physical abuse. After a while, these children think that being a victim is normal, and they expect others to victimize them.

In healthy families, parents respect their children's thoughts and allow their children to be themselves. The parents respect their children's privacy and knock on bedroom doors before they enter. They want the best for their children, but they don't live through them.

Dishonest communication. Certain topics are off limits in the unhealthy family, no matter how badly the children need to talk about them. The children find Mom crying in her bedroom, but she tells them that nothing is wrong. Aunts and uncles may be living in asylums, or siblings may have died in childbirth, but the children never know anything about them.

Conversations that take place in dysfunctional families are not normal. They hang on either end of this continuum:

PASSIVE ————————	ASSERTIVE ————————	AGGRESSIVE
You say nothing.	You say negative things in a firm, yet calm way.	You scream everything.

The healthier a family is, the more the family members communicate in open, honest ways—even when they don't have good feelings about each other. In these moments, they can speak up, yet not blow up. They are approachable. As assertive people, they can say critical things to each other in gentle ways.

Children in healthy families see that their parents admit their mistakes even though it makes the parents vulnerable. This helps the children know that they, too, will make mistakes and survive. But in dysfunctional families, the parents don't often admit their mistakes, so the children conclude that problems are their fault.

Closed-system mentality. In healthy families with an "open system," children get close to other people. They invite other children over to play, they have adult friends such as Boy Scout or Girl Scout leaders and other youth-group leaders. The parents have nothing to hide and are eager to grow as people. The family acts as a semipermeable membrane, with new ideas flowing in and out of it.

The dysfunctional family does not accept new information or ideas. Children know by example not to get close to anyone, especially adults, outside the family. Parents stick with what they've always believed and don't want to hear about books or groups on parenting.

As a result, children know little about what healthy adults are like. Most of their parents' friends tend to be dysfunctional as well, and the children think that the unhealthy behavior they see is normal.

This "closed system" also means that families are careful not to let information out. They keep "family secrets" about "the latest drama at home" and about their parents' unhealthy behaviors.

Tension and nervousness. The stage for poor development is set even from infancy. King Baby parents don't pick up their babies tenderly. They shove them onto the changing table, yank off the diapers, and jerk on the new ones. Even these little ones pick up tense emotional messages. This tension continues through childhood and forges a negative view of life. Sophia had this experience:

> I sat on the bench at the mall and tried to hold back the tears. I knew I should walk away, but I couldn't. I was mesmerized.
>
> I watched a mother going nuts with her four kids. The baby sat in a stroller screaming, and the mom screamed back. The oldest, a boy about ten years old, tried to calm the baby, but he looked confused. One of the other children was pulling out the dirt from one of those tall plants, and the other child was running away. The oldest caught up with him.
>
> I cried because it reminded me so much of the way I had grown up. I felt so scared for those kids. I wanted to pick them up and cuddle them. I wanted to assure the oldest one that the others would be okay. As the little family walked away, I felt that same knot in my stomach that I had felt during childhood. I wondered if they felt the way I used to feel—*Things are better now, but for how long?*

This tension robs kids of their childhood. They lose their tendency to be adventuresome, playful, and curious. It's as if they skip the basic classes in life—Childhood 101 and 102—and are thrust into adulthood prematurely. They cover up this tension by acting like "looking-good kids." If they don't, the parents get angry or fall apart.

Now, as adults, our nervousness abounds. We have to please others; we have to look good; have to be perfect. We try to act like "normal" adults but end up faking it emotionally.

Low self-esteem. Children in dysfunctional families typically possess low self-esteem because they aren't affirmed or respected. They're rarely told, "Good job," and they rarely feel a sense of achievement. Even worse, they may be belittled and criticized no matter how hard they try.

Some children are "underparented," meaning that parents focus little attention on them, either positive or negative. Parents may stay detached because they're so engulfed in their own problems (or compulsions), or because they don't feel confident in their roles. They don't know how to hug or discipline their children, and they're afraid they'll make mistakes, so they don't even try. Other parents don't "attach" to their children because they don't care enough to make the effort. The children raise themselves.

The inconsistency of an unhealthy family can cause even healthy self-esteem to waver in children. As the parents' moods change, so does the child's self-esteem. Danielle remembers her childhood—and her self-esteem—being full of ups and downs:

> When my dad was working and my mother was happy, I could give speeches at school or try out for drill team. I was confident and tried hard.
> When my dad was in one of his angry moods and my mom was crying all the time, I changed. I didn't call my friends or study very hard. I looked for reasons to get out of the house. Many times I jumped on my bike and rode out into the country. The wind blew against my face and dried the tears.

I felt like two people most of the time. Sometimes I was outgoing and carefree; other times I was scared and tired. I longed to grow up and get away.

When I went off to college, I was afraid at first, but then I started talking to people and getting involved in all kinds of groups. My teachers and supervisors rarely came down on me, but when they did, they were calm about it. I felt like a living, breathing person for the first time.

Delayed development. Growing up in a dysfunctional family can affect emotional, intellectual, and social development. Children from alcoholic families have an increased "morbidity risk," meaning that they are psychologically unhealthy.[1] They experience more distress in moods, conformity, relationships, leadership skills, and emotional stability.[2] Other studies show an increase in depression,[3] hyperactivity,[4] aggression,[5] self-esteem,[6] and legal difficulties as children and adults.[7]

The stress of a dysfunctional family also makes it difficult for children to reach their intellectual potential. In a recent study on how stress affects the brain, researchers found that subjecting rats to hormones associated with stress for long periods of time worked against their brains' ability to learn and remember.[8]

That may explain why kids can't concentrate when their parents are screaming at each other. They stop doing their math homework to listen. *What are they arguing about this time?* they wonder. *Will they get a divorce? If they do, will I live with Mom, or Dad?* They're so distracted they miss the math principles they are supposed to be learning.

Stress also affects the ways that children's personalities develop. For example, psychoanalyst Erik Erikson observed that children specialize in certain developmental tasks during specific stages of life. Here is a simplified version of how those tasks and stages correspond:

Developmental Tasks		Stages of Life
POSITIVE ———— NEGATIVE		
Trust ———— Mistrust		Infancy (0–2)
Autonomy ——— Shame & Doubt		Toddlerhood (2–4)
Initiative ——— Guilt		Early School Age (5–7)
Industry ——— Inferiority		Middle School Age (8–12)
Identity ———— Alienation[9]		Adolescence (13–22)

It's possible that when children experience trauma during one of these stages, they don't develop the corresponding developmental task as fully as they should. When we become adults, we find that because of those and other negative childhood experiences, we are lacking to some degree in

- trust (having confidence in the integrity, ability, and goodwill of other people)
- autonomy (feeling comfortably independent)
- initiative (becoming self-starters)
- industry (finishing tasks)
- identity (feeling that we know and like who we are)

For example, when Carol discussed her infancy with her therapist, they talked about how her sense of trust could have begun to erode at that time. Carol remembered that her parents were divorced when she was an infant, so she questioned her mother and found out that her mother and father had argued a lot during that time. The subsequent "silent treatment" they gave each other had extended to Carol as well.

Carol's therapist noted that this was one of the many reasons why Carol had developed a limited and inconsistent sense of trust. Like a newly blossoming flower that has been walked on, Carol had still grown but was wounded. Other growing-up experiences also had taught her not to trust, so that now, as an adult, her sense of trust is limited.

The Search for "Normalcy"

Children are shocked when they stay overnight with friends and find out that some parents don't argue all the time. They're amazed at how quiet—and sometimes fun—life seems. They can barely understand a world that is so genuinely peaceful. They often reach out to these friends to find out what the proper boundaries are in life—what's too personal, what's offensive.

Relatively healthy adults who were raised in dysfunctional families can often point to healthy relatives or neighborhood families who informally "adopted" them. These children saw these caring and open adults as role models that made more sense than their own parents, and copied their behavior.

When children in dysfunctional families experience healthier family interaction, it whets their appetites to be different from their parents. They say things like, "When I grow up, I'm going to be just like. . . ." Little do they know that their bodies and their memories are set up so that they will probably repeat—and perhaps multiply—their parents' behaviors unless they find the path to recovery.

You may be wondering . . .

Q   What if I'm nothing like my King Baby parent?
A   Most of us try to become the opposite of our King Baby parent. We may not have the same outward behaviors, but we have the same inner drives, sadness, and anger. We may switch compulsions, or we may react in the extreme. The parent is critical and authoritarian, so the child grows up to be weak and permissive. It's like changing chairs on the Titanic: we have the same problem of dysfunctionality, only from a different perspective.

CHAPTER 5

Roles That Get Us through Childhood

Mr. and Mrs. Wells are pillars of the church. They attend every service and can always be counted on to help out. Dad is a ruddy-complexioned mail carrier who serves on the church board. Mom, tall and erect, is a homemaker and takes care of the church kitchen. She collects coupons for the children's home and goes behind the church janitor, cleaning the spots he misses.

Even though Mom and Dad have the same values and interest in church, they aren't warm toward each other. Mom often objects to decisions made at church and tells Dad how he ought to change them. "I'm not a wave maker," he tells her, but then he makes a few waves at church to appease her.

Their oldest child, *Melissa,* is following her mother's example. She cleans the house every Saturday and began teaching Sunday school when she was twelve. Melissa makes excellent grades in high school and holds an office in student government. She keeps the other Wells kids in line when her parents attend church meetings at night.

David, the second child, has never liked school. He doesn't like Melissa, either, and tells her she's "stuffy." David refuses to gloss over the conflict he hears behind his parents' closed bedroom doors. He is disgusted by Dad's blind obedience to Mom. He sees their loveless relationship as something he doesn't want in his life. A few years ago, David's friends began wearing gang-style clothes, and David joined them. It looked like a good way to be his own person. It causes confrontations with his parents, but he likes these fights. "At least they take off their Christian masks," says David.

Cindy, the second daughter, also hears all the commotion behind closed doors but chooses to "drop out." Everyone says that Cindy is shy and sweet, but she has few friends. She doesn't bring those few girlfriends around, because Mom is so controlling. Cindy stays in her room a lot, reading and brushing her hair. She did speak up once to ask for a puppy, but Mom wouldn't let her have one because she said that dogs were loud and messy. Dad gave Cindy a parakeet, which she babies and keeps in her room.

Gary, the youngest, sees the hurt ricocheting back and forth among Mom, Dad, and David, and does what he can to remedy it. He often gets between his parents and tries to defend Dad. Occasionally it works, but sometimes Mom accuses Gary of interfering. Once, when Dad brought up divorce, Gary spent the entire evening trying to talk him out of it. Gary likes to ride alone in the car with Dad; it's the only time he sees Dad smile.

Children look for ways to cope with the chaos in their dysfunctional families. They find the consistency that they have missed in their families by adopting a role in childhood that they continue to use even in adult life. The Wells children adopted the following roles.[1]

The Responsible Child
In the midst of chaos, I'll work hard so people will love me.

The oldest child is often overly "responsible" anyway, but in a dysfunctional family it is doubly so. Also called "the hero," the *responsible child* takes care of younger brothers and sisters, as Melissa does. Sometimes responsible children even take care of the parents. At the age of ten, they can tuck the alcoholic parent into bed and make dinner for the whole family.

The responsible child is seven-going-on-fifty-seven. A typical day for this child includes getting an A on a test at school, helping the teacher after school, and doing the laundry when he or she gets home. Parents are proud of this "banner child" for being so mature.

If families like the Wellses come to counseling and are told they are dysfunctional, they object: "How can you say our family is dysfunctional? Look at Melissa. She's a 4.0 student. She's a cheerleader. She's involved in church. Could a dysfunctional family produce a child like this?"

Some responsible children are savvy enough to understand that they're saving face for the family. They may give their counselors faint, lopsided smiles, knowing they've sacrificed their childhoods to help their families function "normally."

When these children become actual adults, they may not want to raise families of their own. Suzanne, the responsible child in an alcoholic family, mothered a younger brother who committed suicide and two younger sisters who got pregnant as teens. Before Suzanne married, she warned her fiancé, "I'm not having children. I already raised one set of kids, and they turned out bad."

In the workplace, responsible adult children are successful but insecure. They may be rigid and controlling, with very little insight into why they do what they do. *Somebody's got to organize the world,* they think. *No one else will.* Tragically, they take the job.

The Acting-Out Child
In the midst of chaos, I'll become the problem
so people will notice me.

Some children act out the pain of their dysfunctional families in aberrant behavior. As a result, they are often the presenting problems when their families seek counseling.

Parents like Mr. and Mrs. Wells say, "David hit the teacher. We don't know what to do about him. We love David, but he has a problem. Fix him so we can be a wonderful family again." That's why the role of the *acting-out child* is also called "the scapegoat."

When the counselor asks the Wells family what a typical night at home is like, David is the one to deliver the straight scoop. He exposes the family's dysfunctionality, and the family gets mad because David has disobeyed the rule of secrecy and has broken open their closed family system. It's no surprise that this child is considered the black sheep of the family.

The dysfunctional family doesn't realize that the acting-out child is running away, starving herself, being sexually permissive, or wrecking cars because of the dysfunctional relationships within the family. These children are consumed with anger at their parents and at the world. They draw attention by their behavior, getting into whatever kind of trouble it takes to do so.

As adults, acting-out children move from relationship to relationship without attaching. They become bored quickly and can't control their impulses or wait for things. They enjoy new and changing environments, so they migrate from place to place, never finding home. Home is a meaningless word. It didn't mean anything in childhood; it doesn't mean anything to the adult.

The typically low frustration tolerance of these children makes them self-destructive. Of all the children, they are the ones most likely to become alcoholic or chemically dependent. If they don't connect with someone who can help them, they have little hope.

Is there good news for ACDFs who are still playing their roles as acting-out children? Yes. These ACDFs have the best chance of getting well, because they understood most clearly the dysfunctionality of their families.

The Adjuster
In the midst of chaos, I'll ignore people
so they won't bother me.

Some children get burned one too many times early in life and never venture out again. They adjust their expectations of their parents because they've learned that they won't get their needs met. "Why try?" is their motto.

Adjusters usually detach themselves from their families. These "lost children," as they are also called, are the "invisible" ones among the children. In the Wells family, Cindy detaches by staying in her room and playing with her parakeet. She's also good at drawing, which is a fitting hobby because it gives her a world into which she can withdraw. She can detach even in the presence of the family as she watches television and never hears the arguing around her.

When adjusters grow up, they still don't trust people. In their own families, they find ways to stay uninvolved. It's difficult for them to live with other people and feel safe. They tuned out for so long that it's now difficult to tune back in, to feel comfortable.

Adjusters often reproduce their family environments and marry those who will keep their lives in an uproar. If situations become too troubled, they do what they've always done: leave. That may mean going from marriage to marriage or from church to church or from job to job, looking for a place to feel comfortable.

The Placater
In the midst of chaos, I'll make people
feel better so they'll love me.

Even when *placaters* are the youngest children in their families, they act as comforters, therapists, and referees for their parents and siblings. They are hypersensitive to the feelings of other people and have learned to "read" people well. They get into the middle of other people's arguments and try to solve them, just as Gary Wells does. When Mom gets upset with Dad, Gary listens to her complaints and then pleads Dad's case to her. His placater role has become so established that the other family members also come to him with problems.

Some placaters "fix" their families by getting them to laugh. This version of a placater is called the "mascot," or "family clown." When the Wells family gets particularly tense, Gary entertains his mother and sisters by coming up with ridiculous ways of taking out the kitchen garbage. If David storms out, Gary distracts his family with a joke or a funny story about school. Other placaters are very serious, though. They get so involved in other people's problems that they don't know how to laugh.

Placaters struggle with codependency. They often get walked on, and they tend to sacrifice themselves to the point that they neglect their own needs. Other people lean on placaters so hard that they often blame the placaters when things go wrong. "That's what you told me to do, and it didn't work!" they say. The vintage placater will take the blame.

As adults, placaters may complain a lot but do little about the problem because they think this is their lot in life. They never learned to have healthy relationships but have encouraged people to victimize them. If they get into relationships in which people want to meet their needs, it feels foreign to them. They may even leave these healthy relationships.

These four roles surprise those who expect children to react to their dysfunctional families by rebelling. Instead, three of the four roles are "looking-good kids," which explains why so many ACDFs *seem* so healthy: adjusters keep the peace, responsible children force peace, and placaters negotiate peace. It's only the acting-out children who disturb the peace.

Uncovering the Real Me

Understanding the roles we played and still play helps us understand why we do the confusing things we do. It helps us see what kinds of masks we wear and what we will have to do to remove them.

Figure out which role you played.   You may feel that you fit primarily into one role and secondarily into another. Some children, especially "only" children, may absorb a little of all the roles or use two at the same time. John, whose father was a minister, was a responsible child at home, at church, and at school with one group of kids. He had another set of friends at school, though, who helped him play the acting-out child by introducing him to drugs. He was never found out, and he grew up to be a "looking-good" responsible adult with a secret sexual addiction. He sometimes confuses his employer by revealing the acting-out child at the wrong time.

What if you don't remember which role you played? It may not be obvious at first. In therapy or support groups, memories may click, and it will come back to you. Perhaps you'll recognize which roles your siblings played, and then you'll see yourself. If you talk in a support group about how you behaved as a child, people can give you feedback on how they see you. Discovering the role you played may shock you. It is similar to hearing your voice on audiotape or seeing yourself on videotape for the first time.

Determine how you are still playing your role.   The logical conclusion is that, once children leave the dysfunctional family, they shed their roles because they don't need them anymore. That isn't how it works.

As adults, we use our childhood roles on our jobs, in our churches, and in our own families. Our new life situations usually don't require this of us, but we feel comfortable in these roles. We have carved these niches for ourselves, and we get stuck there. Here's how Dan continued his childhood role:

Fifteen years ago, my father almost died of cirrhosis of the liver. My three older sisters and I sat for many long hours by his bedside in the hospital. He barely made it through the ordeal. Throughout this stressful time, I, a placater, acted as the family counselor. I listened to my sisters. I reassured one sister that she hadn't failed my dad. I told another how well she had taken care of me. I cheered up the youngest one by telling her all the great qualities she had that were like my dad's. I patted myself on the back for being so "caring" when I felt so bad.

After my sisters and I took Dad home, I felt keyed up. I played basketball at the gym, and I played extra hard. The sweat was rolling down my back, and my socks were soaked. I ran to the shower room.

Once I was alone in the shower, my feelings overcame me. What if my father had died? I felt so afraid and so alone.

I cried uncontrollably like I had never done before in my life. The noise of the shower barely covered up my sobbing. The little boy in me was feeling like he had felt many times as a kid, knowing his father was killing himself with alcohol. There was nothing I could do as a little boy; there was nothing I could do now.

I was crying for myself, too. My role as placater was becoming too lonely a road to follow, but I didn't know how to share my sorrow with my sisters in a healthy way. I desperately needed to talk to them, to tell them how afraid I was, but I couldn't. I had to grieve by myself.

Our roles hamper us in our newer adult relationships as well. We can't stop playing our roles with our spouses and friends. Responsible children often don't let their spouses carry their part of the load. Acting-out children want their spouses to carry it all. "Lost" children won't talk about problems with their friends, and placaters attempt to solve their friends' problems with simplistic solutions.

Seek healthy behavior, not "role" behavior. Knowing our roles shows us what to work on in the recovery process. Responsible children and placaters learn to let others take care of themselves. Adjusters learn to attach and not tune out. Acting-out children learn to attach to other people and use more positive behavior to get their needs met. We become free to discover who we are inside and free to care for others in healthy ways.

Shedding our roles is a lifelong process of making different behavior choices. When we find ourselves acting within our roles, we can stop ourselves and ask, *What is the healthy thing to do? What do I need to do?* We "test the waters" by choosing healthier ways to view ourselves and healthier ways to interact with others, and then we see how those ways work out. Even adjusters and acting-out children find that they want to reach out to others, and they search for healthy ways to do so. Gradually, our old behavior traps fall away.

As difficult as it was for Dan, he called his oldest sister when he got home and told her how broken he felt about his dad. From his recovery he knew that she was the responsible child and would understand better than his other sisters how he tried to take care of people. He knew that she didn't understand everything he was saying, but it was important that he denounce his placater role by sharing his grief.

As each of us uncovers our real selves, we talk to ourselves in a new way: *In the midst of chaos, I will ask God to help me determine what is the healthiest behavior, and I will do it.*

You may be wondering . . .

Q *Do children ever change roles?*

A Roles may change as the children grow up.

You might use one role in your early years and then another in your adolescent years. When the responsible child leaves the nest, another child may fill that vacant spot. The family responds by saying, "Our little one has certainly grown up!"

CHAPTER 6

My Past Lives in Me

We start out the week with the best of intentions, determined to be healthy, happy people. Still, something poisons our activities and relationships. We try to shake it, but we can't.

That "something" is what physician Dr. Hugh Missildine calls the "inner child of the past,"[1] who plays a part in our conversations and relationships.

It's been said that a person is the sum total of his or her experiences. These experiences form the inner child (or child within), whom we cannot ignore. Those who grew up in healthy families have a confident, content inner child that propels them through life, while we as ACDFs have an underdeveloped, injured inner child that holds us back. Our confused and violated inner child does not act and react freely, but stays within one or more dysfunctional family roles.

A large part of ACDF recovery is identifying the feelings of this child within. Then we try to understand how the child within interacts in our adult lives.

The Child Within

The Childlike Part. What is it about children that is so positive? ". . . Unless you change and become like little children, you will never enter the kingdom of heaven. Therefore, whoever humbles himself like this child is the greatest in the kingdom of heaven" (Matt. 18:3, 4).

Childlikeness means being trustful, innocent, and sold out to a parent who believes in you. This playful, hopeful part of us is enthralled with the environment if it's a safe environment. This part is like Samantha, a three-year-old who ACDF Bob talks about:

> Rain or shine, Samantha went out to the curb and built little villages in the mud. She used leaves for boats and stems for trees. She had mud on her arms, on her dress, in her hair. One time she even took off her shoes and let the mud squeeze between her toes.
>
> She was three, and I was seven, and I thought she was stupid. I told her so. Since I was so much more an "adult," I nicknamed her "the Gutter Queen."
>
> I realize now I was jealous of Samantha. She had something in her life I didn't have. She enjoyed herself. She was free to do little-kid things, while I was busy worrying about what would happen when my stepfather got home. I didn't have time to let go and be a kid.
>
> One time Samantha's mom came out, and I got ready to hightail it out of there on my bike. I figured Samantha was going to get it bad. Instead, her mom smiled at me.
>
> Samantha showed her mom the things she had built, and her mom told Samantha that she liked her village. Then she told Samantha to come around to the back door when she wanted to come in so she could get cleaned off with the hose.
>
> Samantha's world was like a foreign country that I could never know anything about.

The "child within" can delight in simple things, even pushing a stick six inches one way and then pushing it back. Children in dysfunctional families aren't relaxed enough to do that. When we played in the mud, our parents said, "Get out of there. You're ruining your clothes."

As children, we didn't understand why we had to stop playing in the mud. We weren't given options such as putting on old clothes and boots. Our fun was simply cut short with no thought of what it meant to us.

Throughout childhood, we had to make elaborate plans to work around parents. Now, as adults, we go to great lengths to find enjoyment. We can't just go to a nearby lake or beach; it isn't "fun" unless we go to an island resort. Even then, "fun" somehow doesn't feel right.

For most of us, this childlike side of ourselves has been hurt so often without receiving comfort that we have almost lost that part. We spend our energy shutting out inadequate feelings and pretending that we are strong enough to overcome it all.

As ACDFs in recovery, we become responsible for rediscovering our trapped child within. We give this child time to explore and enjoy life.

The Childish Part. This part of our child within imitated the King Baby parent. We never learned delayed gratification; we wanted what we wanted when we wanted it.

A legalistic mom or drunken father always demanded more. "Get me a beer!" "Make your bed again, and do it right this time!" Those of us who played the roles of responsible children and placaters kept trying to perform perfectly. After a while, we sensed that our parents didn't know what they wanted at all. Nothing made them happy. Some of us gave up, others kept trying.

Now, as adults, we are horrified to see King Baby erupt within ourselves as well. Yet this is logical when we realize that the lack of bonding with our parents left a pit of emptiness inside us. Our emotional needs weren't met, so now we grab for something—anything—to fill that pit. We are full of anger, rebellion, and deceit; we feel we have to manipulate people to get what we want.

Some of us display this *childish* side most of the time, while others try to hide it. Suddenly, a particularly painful issue arises at work or at a church board meeting, and King Baby explodes. Other people look surprised and wonder what happened.

You may think, *Other ACDFs may act like that, but I don't.*
We're good at keeping King Baby under wrap, reserving
this behavior for our families or inner circles of friends.
Still, you insist, that's not you. But ACDFs who have
never behaved like King Baby may do so during recovery.
That quiet adjuster child refuses to be walked on anymore
and overcompensates by becoming a bully. When this happens to us, it's because we're facing the broken child within
whose needs weren't met—and we're angry about that.
Part of recovery is learning to set limits for the King Baby
inside us.

When ACDFs Get Together

When a person marries, so does the child within. That
means that a marriage brings four people together—the
wife, the husband, the wife's child within, and the husband's child within.[2]

No wonder marriage can be a struggle. We are dealing
with an adult bride and groom and a child bride and
groom. It's often difficult to guess which person is speaking at the moment.

Jean, an ACDF, recognizes how important the inner
child's role is in her marriage:

> Joe and I both were frustrated when we came home
> from work. My boss had yelled at me, and Joe had al-
> most been fired. We both wanted love and comfort. We
> both wanted the other to listen, but instead we kept in-
> terrupting the other with complaints.
>
> I could see my needy inner child—and Joe's too—
> coming forward as we got into a fight. Finally, Joe said
> something that made me see how badly he was hurting,
> so I set aside my inner child and listened to Joe. We
> talked about how he could handle his work situation in
> the future.
>
> When Joe was finished, I told him that I needed

some of his time to get things out of my system, too. This surprised him—and me. Before I began my recovery, I would have allowed Joe to spill his needs but would have kept mine to myself. I've learned that that doesn't work; I also need to talk about my own hurts.

Jean was wise to insist that she also should have time to express the needs of her inner child. In a healthy marriage relationship, comfort goes both ways.

When only one spouse shares hurts, the relationship gets stuck. People like Jean come to marriage counseling and say, "Why did I marry him? Why didn't I see that Joe was nothing but a taker?" It's important to understand the needs and even the worst behaviors of your child within and of your future spouse's child within before getting married. Then you aren't surprised.

For most of us, the child within is so hungry for validation that we look for mates who will meet the needs that our parents didn't meet. (We even carry this "parent quest" into work and social relationships, but we do it particularly with mates.) Some of us know we're doing it. Linda's dad had never held a steady job, so Linda looked for a husband who was hard-working and ambitious. Her husband, Mark, hated how his mother had screamed at him daily, so he found in Linda a quiet, nurturing wife to mother him. Never mind that Linda and Mark had nothing in common with each other. They reacted so strongly against their parents that they didn't marry as wisely as they could have.

Others of us don't know how drastic our needs are until we are already married. Many of us "need somebody" desperately because we are so afraid of abandonment. This takes shape in many ways, as it did in Ann's life:

> When Steve told me that he planned to go to the movies with the guys, I felt left out. But I didn't want to be a nag, so I acted as if nothing were wrong.

But that night, when Steve was gone, I remembered the abandonment I had felt when my father was out drinking. When I was eleven, someone tried to break into our house. My mother and I turned on all the lights in the house and grabbed a baseball bat. We sat on the floor of the hallway next to the phone until the police came. We had no idea where my father was. When he came home, we told him about it, and he shrugged his shoulders.

What if someone tried to break in now? I kept wondering. Steve would be gone when I needed him. In my mind, I confronted him with the many times that he had not been there when I needed him. Actually, he was quite innocent in those situations, but my feelings of abandonment were on a roll, and I couldn't stop them. Finally, I went to bed early, hoping I would feel better the next day.

But I didn't. I wanted to get back at Steve for "abandoning" me, so I invited Peggy, a co-worker that Steve didn't like, to dinner. When Peggy showed up, and Steve was angry, I looked blank and asked, "Didn't I tell you Peggy was coming?"

Ann knew that her feelings of being abandoned by Steve were unwarranted, but she couldn't seem to stop feeling them. Her feelings won, and she found a way to get back at Steve by inviting Peggy to dinner. It was too much of a risk to trust Steve, to trust God to take care of Steve, and to trust that she would survive if Steve never came back.

This doesn't mean that marriages between ACDFs are doomed. It means that we each need to understand our own inner child and our spouse's inner child. What are we most afraid of? What are we grasping for? The more completely that couples can answer these questions, the better they'll know how to solve problems.

Another dilemma that we as ACDFs encounter in marriage is that, even though we search for spouses who are not like our parents, we end up marrying that kind of person anyway. This is reflected by the fact that adult children of alcoholics often marry those who are substance abusers.[3] It's as if our inner child is comfortable in dysfunctional relationships and subconsciously seeks them out.

The best way to avoid these dilemmas is to begin our recovery before we marry or choose our mates. Then, two people who are working toward wholeness can build a relatively healthy relationship.

You may be wondering . . .

Q Isn't "inner child" a New Age concept?

A The term *inner child* did not originate with the New Age movement but has been used by psychologists since the 1930s. It usually refers to the intellect and the emotions. As Christians, we believe that the inner child (or child within) includes our spirits as well, because dysfunctionality affects the way we view God. The New Age community uses many psychological and spiritual terms, but that does not taint the words themselves.

Q What if I'm seriously dating a man from a dysfunctional family?

A It's important to ask the following questions. Ideally, your answers to these are yes.

   1. Does he recognize his dysfunctional background?
       If not, encourage him to read a book about dysfunctionality or to attend an ACDF meeting. ACDFs who aren't in recovery don't understand how much havoc their past creates within them or its potential for ruining future relationships.
       Stay away from serious relationships in which your date flatly denies that he or his parent is dysfunctional when something such as alcoholism is apparent to you. (We assume that you are reading and learning enough about dysfunctionality to un-

derstand that not everyone you meet is a work-aholic, a controller, or an abuse victim.)

2. *Is he willing to investigate how his dysfunctional background may affect him now?*
   If not, he may be a victim of his own pride and a potential trap for you. Being in a healthy relationship involves doing whatever recovery work is necessary to learn to express needs and to set boundaries. If he doesn't understand the needs of his child within, he will probably expect you to meet them if you marry him. This would be unfair, of course, because no one can meet the needs of another person's inner child.

   You will know that he is willing to work on his recovery if he will regularly go to a support group or to therapy. Understand that no matter how much recovery you have, your relationship with him cannot take the place of the help he would receive in those settings. It's better to wait to get married until he has worked through at least part of this process.

3. *Are you certain that you didn't seek him out because he's from a dysfunctional family?*
   Even though our conscious minds would disagree, most of us seek to duplicate the tone of our parents' relationships (remember the ACA statistic). Examine your own motives and needs. Is the relationship characterized by honest communication of feelings, or by caretaking, tension, and a violation of boundaries? Would you be dating this man if you felt more secure in God's love and in your own self-worth?

Section 2

The Problems
of Our Present

CHAPTER 7

Scrambling To Be Adults

Can you imagine building cabinets and finding that you have no hammer, no screwdriver, not even a saw? Or suppose you need to make cupcakes for your daughter's birthday, yet you have no cake mix, flour, or eggs? Furthermore, imagine that in both cases it isn't possible to go out and buy what you're missing. You have to substitute with what you already have.

"I can't!" you protest. "I don't have the right materials!"

ACDFs face a similar predicament. Even as adults, our handicapped child within forces us to "make do" without the necessary life skills. We may have compensated by going to college so that we could get good jobs, but now we can't process the criticisms we receive in performance reviews. We work at being witty, and we buy the right clothes so that we can attract our potential spouses, but we can't open up to them after we get married. It puzzles us why other people seem to express their feelings, have fun, and set boundaries easily, while we "wing it" through life.

Those who counsel ACAs paint a clearer picture of these feelings of being lost, with the following thirteen characteristics[1] (which are true for ACDFs from nonalcoholic homes as well). These characteristics help us see that we have not left our dysfunctional families behind, but that their residue continues to contaminate us and our relationships even in our adult lives.

Not every ACDF displays all these characteristics. In our first chapter, Donna described the typical experience of having seven characteristics jump off the page immediately. If you discuss these characteristics in support groups, a few of the more subtle ones may become apparent.

Characteristics of ACDFs

Alienation

We guess at what healthy behavior is.[2]   ACDFs are often confused about how to behave "normally." Other adults don't stamp their feet and march out of the room when they don't get their way, and they think it's silly when we do it. They refuse to let people talk to them as if they were dirt. They don't assume that the worst possible thing will happen in every circumstance. Yet we do these things or allow them to happen because that's how things were in our unhealthy families.

It's not unusual for an ACDF to call a recovering friend and say, "I know that what I want to do is not good, but what is the healthy thing to do?" In some cases, we simply don't know. Healthy behavior is like a foreign language to us.

We usually feel we're different from other people.   As children, we noticed that our families weren't like other families. Ours seemed less capable. We felt left out, as if everyone else got the punch line of a joke and we didn't. Deep inside, we were afraid that we were the joke.

Sometimes our parents' addictive behavior embarrassed us. We knew the neighbors pitied us for the way our moms drank or the way our dads carried on in the driveway.

Carlos remembers feeling that way.

I was playing well in one of my high school basketball games when I saw my father come in. I could tell by the way he walked that he was drunk. I hoped he would sit down and be quiet, but he didn't.

I kept watching him to make sure he didn't embarrass me in front of my friends. I didn't realize how nervous I was until I missed an easy shot out on the court. Then my dad stood up in the stands and yelled, "You're no son of mine."

I wanted to die. There, in front of my friends, their parents, and the school staff, my father made a fool of himself and me. Now everybody knew my dad was a drunk. I couldn't get away, so I tried to stare straight ahead and keep playing. But I caught a few of the guys on the team looking at me as if I were from another planet. Even though no one said anything to me, I felt the distance.

That was fifteen years ago, and now my dad is sober. I'm still working through my anger over it, though. I still tense up when I think someone's going to embarrass me. I never feel like "one of the guys."

We carry this stigma into our adult years. We feel shame even when no one knows our family secrets. We search for answers to our depression. It seems as if everyone else has a formula we don't have. At times it seems as if healthier persons have a magic potion that solves everything. Many of us even became Christians hoping that faith would instantly transform us into happy, controlled, "normal" people.

We fear abandonment. We learned early in life that, even though people said they were available to help us, they weren't. Our King Baby parents were too obsessed with themselves or with their compulsions to be fully present, and our codependent parents had their hands full taking care of the King Baby parents.

As children, we may have heard parents make comments that made us feel that they were going to abandon us through divorce, suicide, or even murder. Even when we knew these were idle threats, we replayed them in our minds and imagined what it would be like if one of our parents left or if we came home to discover a parent that was dead. Grandparents, in some cases, were forced to abandon us as our parents put them on the "blacklist."

As a result, we have become adults who are either *hyper-*dependent (too dependent) or *hypo*dependent (too isolated). We don't know how to find balance. Margaret can't handle problems on her own, so she prods, nags, and almost coerces other people into solving her problems. Craig, however, never consults anyone about a problem. He learned as a child that he would keep his problems to himself if he were smart. As far as he's concerned, he has no problems.

This hypodependency extends even to God. Although we may lead Bible studies, we don't trust God in our heart of hearts. We hide this distrust and act as if our lives are humming along, which is why we never feel the need to get help. If we keep up the facade, our spiritual lives either plateau or burn out.

We struggle with intimate relationships.   Some of us fear abandonment so much that we refuse to form relationships at all. We can go through college and never befriend our roommates. That person on your block who no one knows is probably an ACDF who doesn't attach to people because of fear.

Many of us use that "looking-good kid" image so well that others think they know us when they don't. When they realize we don't ever open up to them, they feel cheated. Maureen didn't even realize she was holding herself back.

> Carol and I were best friends, I thought. I went over to her house all the time. People at church teased us about being twins. Whatever project Carol worked on, everyone knew I was close behind.

Carol called me one night and told me about a problem she was having with her husband. I reminded her that my husband and I had gone through the same thing, and I told her that her faith in God would take care of it. She distanced herself from me after that, and I was hurt.

She later told me that she hadn't wanted me to counsel her that night. She just wanted to cry. I was so used to "fixing" people that I hadn't listened to her.

As we hashed this out, she told me her other problem with me: I never showed her my real self. I never admitted my problems to her until they were over. I always seemed to be on top of things. "You're not real, and I don't feel comfortable around you," she told me.

How could I tell Carol that I was broken inside most of the time? Why couldn't I trust this dear person with my secret anxieties? I never imagined that she wanted that from me. No one else had ever listened to me or wanted to get that close to me. It's always been easier to hold back a little of myself.

Maureen's experience is common. As children, we never saw our parents truly connect with each other, and now we don't know how that works. We were never allowed to share our feelings honestly, and now we don't know how to do that without blowing everyone away.

We get our kudos in relationships from helping other people. We drop everything to listen to someone else's woes and give advice. When it comes to letting them help us, we can't ask them, because when we were young and asked for help, nobody listened.

Some of us struggle with intimate relationships because we also create chaos in them. When things go too well, it feels wrong. We're used to periodic blowups and misunderstandings in our dysfunctional families, so now we cause trouble to make things uncomfortable again. We're "hooked on drama," and it's the only way we feel comfortable.

Recovery from alienation requires that we crawl out of our shells and reach out to "safe" people. We find that other people have these feelings of alienation, too. In support groups, especially, we forge bonds with others who have felt like outsiders throughout their lives. We slowly find "normal" ways to solve problems. We reach out to God and to others until that closeness feels as natural as our alienation once did.

Self-Condemnation

We judge ourselves without mercy.   We have harsh opinions of ourselves and become our own worst critics. We don't give ourselves a break—every infraction is a death-row issue. We criticize ourselves endlessly, and we expect others to do the same thing.

Brent began condemning himself as a child:

> When I played games with other kids on my block and at school, I was too busy judging myself to fully enter into the game. I worried about being overweight and how people might judge me.
>
> If we ran up a hill during a game, I didn't think about getting to the top. I worried about how I looked to the people behind me. I guessed that others judged me, and I amplified people's criticisms. I took my emotional person to the Supreme Court.
>
> As I got older, I worked at losing weight, and I did. But even now, as an adult, I focus more on my appearance than on anything else. I'm still worried that I don't look right, that people are making fun of me.

We seek approval and affirmation.   We have condemned ourselves so much that we constantly need reassurance. We often transfer our need for approval from our parents to other people, especially to employers. Will they affirm us? Will they give us raises? Will we get the plum assignments?

That desire for approval makes us good at reading people. We spent our childhoods saving our own skins. We studied the King Baby parent's face—eye movement, quivering lips—so that now we sense details that others miss. We can tell what people are thinking just by their expressions. That's why so many of us work in the helping professions and are so skillful there.

We are loyal, even to people who hurt us.   We learned loyalty as children, since we helped to keep the family secrets. Now, as adults, we stay in poor relationships and situations when others would not. We may even come back for more. Belinda's story speaks to this problem:

> I get into job situations where people dump on me. My boss cusses at me and tells me to find things I've supposedly lost. When I find them, and it's obvious that *he* lost them, he doesn't apologize. He just says, "Oh, yeah."
>
> Someone suggested that I quit. I can't quit, because I keep thinking that I can change him, that I'm a good influence on him. Something inside me drives me to stick things out, no matter how hopeless they seem.
>
> It's the same with my father. When I talk with him on the telephone, I let him say things about me that aren't true—exaggerations, innuendos. The other day, I stood up for myself when he blew something out of proportion. He got mad and hung up. I felt guilty for a week. I almost called him and apologized, except that I've promised my support group that I won't. I'm practicing for the day I can say to him, "I won't allow you to talk to me that way."

We're slow to stand up for ourselves. We even put ourselves into unsafe circumstances, such as riding with friends who are drunk while driving. Somehow the victim role is comfortable.

Recovery from self-condemnation means that we give ourselves a break. We stop nit-picking at our behavior, and we appreciate our successes, however small they may be. We realize that "beating ourselves up" won't do any good, so we don't do it anymore. We focus on what God leads us to do and less on what will please others. We don't allow ourselves to be victimized. Instead, we seek healthy situations and "go where the love is," as the AA slogan says.

Tension

We have a difficult time having fun. As children, we used to sit on the porch and blow bubbles until we heard the arguments begin in the house. Then we either listened fearfully from the steps or fled to the corner of the yard so we couldn't hear. Either way, we forgot the bubbles and put up our guard.

Now, as adults, we don't know how to have fun. We try to follow the cues of our culture, but it doesn't work. Since our friends say that a fun-filled vacation means seeing the sights, we plan to see every tree and mudhole in just four days. If we can check off every item in the tour book, that will mean we had fun. We'll be able to prove to ourselves that we had fun, because it will be written in black and white on the page. Otherwise, we're never sure if we had fun.

We can't handle free time easily. Unstructured time means we have time to think, which can be unpleasant for people like us, who tend to be depressed anyway. The free time on weekends can be especially difficult, so we structure our free time until none of it's free.

We take ourselves too seriously. We protect ourselves to the point that we go overboard in defending ourselves. We're so lacking in self-esteem that even a little criticism cuts us down. The paradox is that we are the ones who cut ourselves down the most. We exaggerate our offenses and assume we'll suffer the worst possible consequences.

Here's an example of how Jan took life too seriously even as a child:

> As a fourth-grader, I was caught talking with my friend Rhonda when we were supposed to be working. I felt guilty because I liked my teacher so much and wanted to please her. The teacher corrected us in a winsome way, but I took it hard. Rhonda giggled.
>
> Then the teacher said, "At least Rhonda giggled. Jan just looked at me as if she had seen a horror show." The class laughed, but I didn't.
>
> I was confused. Wasn't it terrible to be caught talking? Why did Rhonda laugh? Wasn't I supposed to be repentant when I was wrong?
>
> Over twenty years later, I still remember how upset I was. I see now that the teacher felt sad that I had taken it so hard. She tried to get me to lighten up.
>
> To this day, I'm mortified when I make a mistake. I marveled at a friend who laughed when she forgot the words as she sang the special music at church. The congregation even laughed with her. If that had happened to me before I began recovery, I probably would have cried on the platform. Now I could keep going but would cry later. Someday I hope to be able to laugh about my mistakes.

We have difficulty following a project through from beginning to end. The tension and chaos were so great in our childhoods that we didn't finish homework or extracurricular projects as kids. We may have seen our King Baby parents begin many things with great fanfare, but there was little follow-through.

As adults, we still don't finish things, or we put them off until the last minute. We function well only if someone is standing over us.

Some of us overreact by becoming superresponsible.[3] We vow that we'll be different, and we go overboard to prove ourselves. We find that we enjoy being superresponsible, since we don't trust others to follow through anyway. We assume they'll abandon us or forget our project, so it's much safer if we're in charge.

Recovery from tension means that we teach our minds to shut off the panic button in situations that seem to re-create our past. We loosen up and lighten up. This is evidenced by the laughter that occurs in support groups as we reflect on our unhealthy characteristics. This laughter is a step toward honesty and healing as we say, "Yeah, that's the way I am, and it's sure not healthy." We accept the absurdity of our dysfunctional behavior, and we work on changing it.

Distrust

We overreact to changes over which we have no control. Learning that we have a new supervisor or a mysterious health problem has been a signal to panic. We jump to the worst conclusion and make elaborate plans to change things back to the way they were. Others accuse us of being too rigid, and tell us to "go with the flow," to be flexible.

Some ACDFs demonstrate this characteristic by becoming commandos in relationships. If we think someone is attacking us verbally, we're quick to defend ourselves with a destructive verbal raid or an evasive maneuver. We protect ourselves at all costs.

At the core of this problem is the desire to control our environments. We don't want to be put into the same hurtful situations in which we suffered as children. During childhood, we survived by controlling: we kept family members from fighting, we amused the cantankerous person, we urged others to exit at the right time—or we managed to exit ourselves. As adults, life is too complex to try to control our world the way we did as children.

We lie when it would be just as easy to tell the truth.   In dysfunctional families, we learned that open communication didn't work and that lying kept us out of trouble. Bending the truth diverted the wrath of the King Baby parent. Now, as adults, we lie to stay out of trouble, or we exaggerate our troubles so that we can get sympathy. If we're ultra—"looking-good kids," we exaggerate to impress others with how well we handle problems.

Sandra shows us an example of the difficulty of open communication.

> While visiting my in-laws, I stayed in my sister-in-law's old room and found a beautiful pink scarf, which my sister-in-law had obviously discarded when she moved out years ago. I knew the scarf would look great with a dress I had just bought, so I put it into my suitcase. I told myself that I would ask my mother-in-law later if I could have it.
>
> If I had asked my mother-in-law about it, she probably would have said, "That old thing? Take it." But I couldn't ask her, even though she is a generous, optimistic person. I couldn't risk rejection, no matter how far-fetched it seemed.

We lock ourselves into certain courses of action without giving serious consideration to alternative behaviors or consequences. Sometimes we make impulsive decisions, such as breaking up with someone, on a whim. We can't explain why we must, but our feelings are overwhelming us, so we must do it now. Then we're sorry later.

After we get burned a few times in doing this, we may abandon our impulsiveness and become more analytical than ever. We research decisions, which become increasingly difficult to make as we juggle our desire to please, our self-criticism, and our overresponsibility. We feel stressed out from turning things over and over in our minds.

Recovery from distrust involves surrendering to God our need to control. We understand that God has not abandoned us and that he is worthy and able to direct our lives. We trust others enough to tell the truth about how we feel, what we want, what we think about others. We sort out mixed motives and emotions in support groups and journals, and then present ourselves as we are. We listen to others with open minds, relieved that we finally can depend on others without having to figure everything out for ourselves.

Learning about these characteristics clears up the mysteries of our adult behavior. As we walk through life and recall these characteristics, it's common to have "aha!" moments, in which we think, *So that's why I behave the way I do!*

You may be wondering . . .

Q *Why is control so unhealthy? Isn't self-control a fruit of the Spirit (Gal. 5:22, 23)?*

A It's not that control is always bad—only when it's used excessively. Often our preoccupation with control disturbs our peace of mind ("What if . . . ?"), or we use it to manipulate others. Our desire to control develops into a closed system so that we don't consider new ideas and we have ten reasons why no one else's solutions will work. We work so hard at controlling our environments that we no longer surrender circumstances, people, and problems to God.

CHAPTER 8

Blurred Spiritual Vision

How do you picture God? Have you ever seen him as

- a Santa Claus, who rewards us only if we're good?
- a detached Father Time, who isn't available?
- a cosmic prison guard, who watches every move?
- the Wicked Witch of the West (from *The Wizard of Oz*), who is out to get us?
- a fair-weather friend, who abandons us when illness or trouble darkens our lives?

To have grown up in a dysfunctional family is to view life through smoked glass. Nothing is bright and clean. Even our views of God are tinged so that we see him as distant and unfair. Sure, we know that the Bible says that God is love, but we don't believe it in our hearts.

Some of us feel a terrible alienation from God. Here's how Randy describes it:

> I feel a million miles away from God, as if he doesn't care about me or understand my needs. I pray, and it seems as if God doesn't answer. Even when I use the phrases "Thy will be done" or "In Jesus' name," it doesn't work. When I have troubles, God doesn't step in and take care of them. Nothing ever seems to get better.
>
> Faith is especially hard. I can't see God. What I want is for him to hold me. I want to be able to call on him and have him appear in my room and sing me to sleep, but he doesn't. So this means I have to trust that he cares, but I don't trust anyone. Sometimes I wonder if God is really there at all.

Parents: Our Clues About God

Part of the reason for this alienation from God is that he is spirit, and we don't see him physically present on earth. This physical presence is extremely important to children, so as kids we looked to our parents for "hugs from God." If they didn't hug us, we wondered if God loved us.

Since we could see our parents, and they seemed to be all-powerful, godlike people, many of us assumed that God was like our parents. If our parents were sensitive to us and took time for us, we saw God as one who listens and who takes time.

If the compulsive parent in our families was a promise breaker or a legalistic scorekeeper, we may have figured that God was the same way. If Dad was mean, God must be mean, too. If Mom was too busy for me, so was God.

Many times our parents' meanness or inattentiveness was unintentional. They were distracted by alcohol or some other compulsion and didn't give us the time we needed. Yet the result is the same: our image of God was tainted by our parents' problems.

David Seamands points out, in his book *Healing of Memories*, how the hurts of our past can distort our views of God in the following ways:

The Way God Really Is	*The Way We See Him*
loving & caring	hateful & unconcerned
good & merciful	mean & unforgiving
steadfast & reliable	unpredictable & untrustworthy
unconditional grace	conditional approval
present & available	absent when needed
giver of good gifts	takes away, "kill joy"
nurturing & affirming	critical & unpleasable
accepting	rejecting
holy, just & fair	unjust, unfair & partial[1]

We heard, of course, in church about "the way God really is"—how he didn't have the dysfunctional characteristics of our parents—yet we didn't sense it in our hearts. Now, as adults, it's as if there's a traffic jam between our minds and our hearts. Our minds believe that God is love, but our hearts won't go along with it.

Here's how Jan describes this problem:

> Every time something went wrong, I felt as if God were picking on me, that he was mad at me. It could have been something even as trivial as a broken faucet or misplaced insurance forms, and I would feel that God was working against me. With each trial I experienced, I became more hardened against God. I developed a spiritual chip on my shoulder, expecting problems at every turn.
>
> The worst part of it is that I knew in my mind that God wasn't like that. I had taught Bible studies for many years and had written dozens of Bible-school lessons. I searched the Scripture for passages about God's love and studied them over and over. I tried so hard to make my heart believe them, but I kept responding to God as if he were a punishing, stingy tyrant. I could have won a debate defending God's love, but I still felt deep inside as if he were picking on me.

In our confusion, we try to hide our negative thoughts from God, as if God can't read them anyway! We argue with ourselves, saying, "God loves me! He's wonderful!" but we don't believe it. We quote Scriptures about God's love, as everyone tells us to do, but it doesn't solve the problem. Much of our recovery work includes getting the truths about God through that traffic jam and into our hearts.

"Looking-Good" Christians

If we attended church as children, we learned early how to handle this distortion around church people. First of all, we didn't let the teaching we received there cancel out the distorted image we were seeing through the smoked glass of our dysfunctional families. Our parents' everyday examples carried more weight than the weekly church teaching. In some instances, we heard at church only about God's anger and not his love, which further warped our views of God.

We accepted this God-parent distortion as yet another mixed message in our lives. As children in dysfunctional families, we were used to mixed messages. At home, Dad and Mom may have yelled at each other hatefully, only for Mom to tell us, "We really love each other." The "truth" that we experienced was that they hated each other; the words we heard were that they loved each other. We learned early in life to "listen" to actions and disregard words.

We became "looking-good kids" at church by pretending that what the church said about God was true. We parroted the right phrases: at home, "Sure, my parents love each other"; at church, "Sure, God loves me." We pretended and even wanted to believe that the good things we heard about God were true, but it didn't seem likely.

This pretense didn't occur on a conscious level as children, so now, as adults, we're shocked to find that we've developed an unintentional phoniness in our faith. We go to church, we sing hymns, we quote Scripture, but we never know how to be genuine with God. We are afraid he will abandon us or mistreat us.

If you grew up in a dysfunctional yet "respectable church family," the distortion about God may be even greater. You may have felt that the church leaders "sanctioned" your dysfunctional family, even though they didn't know how dysfunctional it was. This confirmed your worst fears that the church was just like your family: an unsafe place to talk, to trust, or to feel. Acting-out children especially may have wondered, *If God is so smart, why do my parents fool those people at church? Why won't someone at church help me?*

Distorting Scripture

Our dysfunctionality distorts not only the way we view God but also the way we interpret Scripture. The hurts of our past can trip us up so that we view Scripture through the smoked glass of our dysfunctional families' ways. Here are some common distortions:

Being good enough.   We turn the Good News into Bad News as we misinterpret the Bible to say that we are no good or that Christians have to work tirelessly to please God. We reason that we're so bad that "the peace that passes all understanding" must have passed us by. Says ACDF Bill:

> I could quote all those verses about working out your own salvation, but I couldn't quote the ones about God's love. The verses that seem to emphasize how guilty I was as a Christian were the ones that motivated me. They scared me to death. I was convinced that the only way God would love me was if I kept working for him.

In recovery, we learn the difference between playing people-pleasing games with God and surrendering our whole selves to him. We learn that the surrender of our whole selves (including the hurts and mistakes) makes obedience come more easily: "Come to me, all you who are weary and burdened, and I will give you rest. Take my yoke upon you and learn from me, for I am gentle and humble in heart, and you will find rest for your souls. For my yoke is easy and my burden is light" (Matt. 11:28–30). We connect with others, instead of riding solo in the strong and sturdy John Wayne style of Christianity. We admit our own powerlessness and depend on God to help us with his divine power. We focus on God's righteousness, instead of on our own righteousness, or lack of it.

"Love thy neighbor"? We often misinterpret sermons and Bible verses about loving our neighbors as commands to be codependent. We think we're supposed to give in to the King Baby whims of other people even when it harms us.

In recovery, we learn that *agape* love can be patient but tough. In the Old Testament, God loved the nation of Israel even though she worshiped idols and practiced human sacrifice. He gave her many chances to repent through the prophets he sent. Yet God did not allow himself to be abused when Israel ignored his warnings. The northern kingdom was scattered forever, and the slightly less wicked southern kingdom was taken into captivity and was then returned to her homeland.

We learn to copy God's ways. He's not only patient and loving, but also firm and discerning: "Each of us should please his neighbor *for his good,* to build him up" (Rom. 15:2, emphasis ours). It doesn't do King Baby parents any good to continue to speak hurtfully to us. The most loving way to *build up* that parent is by "speaking the truth in love" (Eph. 4:15): "I love you, Dad, but I will not allow you to speak to me that way."

Instant joy and peace? Since ACDFs tend to be tense, and even depressed, the following verses are ripe for misinterpretation:

> Rejoice in the Lord always. I will say it again: Rejoice! . . . Do not be anxious about anything, but in

everything, by prayer and petition, with thanksgiving, present your requests to God. And the peace of God, which transcends all understanding, will guard your hearts and your minds in Christ Jesus. Finally brothers, whatever is true, whatever is noble, whatever is right, whatever is pure, whatever is lovely, whatever is admirable—if anything is excellent or praiseworthy— think about such things. (Phil. 4:4, 6–8)

Curt, like many ACDFs, latched onto these verses as a quick ticket to happiness, but then resented them because they seemed so impossible.

I never felt like rejoicing. It's hard to rejoice when you've never seen it modeled. I wondered if there were a secret to this rejoicing: *Maybe if I pray, read Scripture, or perform the right ritual, I can rejoice and have peace.*

As I began ACDF recovery, it got worse. I felt that the phrase "think about these [positive] things" meant that if I shut out the pain of my past and ignored my upbringing, I would be okay. I had already tried that— it's called denial—and it hadn't worked. It reminded me of a parent who spanks you unjustly and then says, "Now smile." I knew that facing my pain was helping me recover. Why was the Bible saying otherwise?

In recovery, we realize that rejoicing in the Lord isn't the same as "being up." This rejoicing often occurs in the midst of pain—Paul was writing these words from his prison cell, for example. We learn that, by loving God and focusing on him, we can praise him even when everything else looks hopeless.

We discover that joy and peace are time-released capsules, not instant uppers. In our recovery, we have to focus on "whatever is true" by facing past hurts in order to focus on more positive, "lovely" things.

Legalistic formulas. As masters of self-condemnation, we use Bible verses to beat ourselves over the head. Almost any passage can make us feel guilty. Jan used to feel guilty when she read the preceding passage in Philippians.

"Rejoicing in the Lord" was an achievement far beyond me. This was "advanced Christianity," reserved for special people, and I was a second-class Christian. I was hopeless. Depression had hovered over me my entire life, and I didn't think I could ever "rejoice in the Lord always."

I was so desperate for peace that I turned verses 6 and 7 into a spiritual formula:

Step 1: Work hard at rejoicing.
Step 2: Pray.
Step 3: Wait for peace to land in my lap.

It was like using a facial—spread it on, let it dry for ten minutes, wash it off, and you have perfect skin. It sounds silly that I did that, but it's the most normal thing in the world for a depressed ACDF. We're always looking for new formulas; we read all the latest self-help books.

As I ventilated my hurt and anger, that daily depression lifted. I still don't rejoice in the Lord *always,* but I've tasted joyfulness. God's joy and peace creep up on me more and more, and replace the inner chaos. From talking with more mature Christians, I see that rejoicing in the Lord is tough even for them. Once again, I was judging myself without mercy.

I've quit using Scripture as a spiritual hickory switch to beat myself up with. It's much easier to grow in God, to rest in his peace, when I'm not clamoring so much for it.

In recovery, we trust God to work in our lives instead of feeling driven to achieve what we think of as spiritual success.

Instant righteousness? Another scriptural concept that may confuse ACDFs is that of being "a new creation" in Christ. Second Corinthians 5:17 says, "Therefore, if anyone is in Christ, he is a new creation; the old has gone, the new has come!" Well-meaning Christians may tell the ACDF, "This Scripture means that you are released from your sin nature, and your past shouldn't bother you."

Becoming a new creation (some versions say "new creature") in Christ isn't an instant process. This lengthy process is described in John 8:32: "Then you will know the truth, and the truth will set you free." Bible teacher Dr. Lawrence Richards says about this passage, "To 'know' the truth is not to intellectually comprehend, but to experience. To know the 'truth' is not to focus on a body of knowledge, but to live in touch with reality as God knows reality."[2]

This explanation helps us understand our problem. First, we will "know," or experience, the truth when we get it through the traffic jam between our hearts and our minds. Second, "reality" as God knows reality is that he loves us. The more we experience this truth, the freer we are to become "new creatures in Christ."

Violated promises? We also look skeptically at Bible verses that promise God's protection, especially if we were abused. We question verses such as these:

> For he will command his angels concerning you
> to guard you in all your ways;
> they will lift you up in their hands,
> so that you will not strike your foot against a stone." (Ps. 91:11–12)

"If this verse were true," the ACDF asks, "where were those angels when I needed them? Why was my childhood so filled with fear?"

These verses tell us that God provides angelic protection as he thinks it is needed. They don't promise that Christians will never have problems or will never suffer unfairly (which is what we often want them to say). If these verses did promise complete protection, no believer would ever have stubbed a toe on a stone! Not only is this conclusion ridiculous, but we know that many of the early Christians were persecuted (Acts 8:1–3) and that at least one apostle, James, was beheaded (Acts 12:2).

When it looks as if God has violated a promise to us, it's wise to examine the main point of the Bible passage. Are we searching for what the text actually says, or are we putting promises into God's mouth?

Part of our problem with verses such as Psalms 91:11–12 is that we want to know why God does what he does. Since God provides protection as *he thinks it is needed,* why didn't he give us more protection, be it angelic or human?

This is part of the human struggle to understand God and his decisions. Trying to understand God is not a recommended goal or a practical one, because he knows all and we'll just become frustrated in trying (Isa. 40:13). Instead, our goal is to know God and love him. As we do so, we find peace even with the things we don't understand. We may still question him at times, but we do so in order to know him and love him.

These examples of easily misinterpreted Scripture show how we funnel our theology through our dysfunctional family experiences. Recovery means wiping the smoked glass clean and relearning the intent of Scripture. We understand each verse in the context of other biblical passages, and we quit beating ourselves up with isolated proof-texts.

Understanding Scripture better relieves some of our struggle. For years, we've tried to obey all the commands we've heard from pulpits, because we wanted to give our all to God. Yet our feelings were so far removed from those ideas that obedience seemed impossible.

In recovery, we finally understand more of "reality as God knows reality":

- that God loves us and declares us "good enough";
- that his love isn't based on our perfect obedience;
- that he equips us to love others in healthy ways;
- that he knows our thoughts—including our evil thoughts—and loves us anyway;
- that he keeps all his promises, even when we don't understand how he's keeping them.

With this understanding, it's easier to get out of God's way so that he can help us grow.

You may be wondering . . .

Q *Where can I find correct images of God?*
A Meditate on passages in the Bible that picture God's love. Parables are helpful because stories can weave their way through that mind-to-heart traffic jam when facts can't. They help us "know" the truth by experiencing it vicariously.

Here are a few parables that stress God's love:

- The persistent owner of the vineyard (Matt. 21:33–41).
- The shepherd in the parable of the lost sheep, who risks everything to find the one lost lamb (Luke 15:3–7).
- The prodigal son's father, who must have been watching diligently to have seen his son a long way off. Like that father, God searches us out, and he fully blesses us when we come to him (Luke 15:20, 22).

It is also enlightening to read through the Psalms and search for signs of God's character. Psalms 103:8ff. says that God is compassionate and slow to anger. Yet we don't simply quote these to ourselves; we pray them to God, even in the midst of our hurt and anger.

CHAPTER 9

Religious Myths
That Sabotage Recovery

As we peer through the smoked-glass windows of our dysfunctional backgrounds, the Christian life also loses its luster and meaning. Our dark and dusty images of God and our misinterpretations of Scripture strangle our faith. We can no longer stand the phoniness of our faith, so we either leave the church or adopt a "looking-good Christian" profile. This is how Curt felt this tension:

> Throughout my Christian life, I professed that God loved me. I believed in my mind that God was there, but I secretly wondered why a loving God hadn't protected me from the chaos of my upbringing. I had a split faith: I claimed a victory in Christ, but I had secret doubts.
>
> Once, when I told a pastor about my doubts, he questioned my salvation. He said I must be harboring some sin in my life. When I told another Christian, she gave me a book on prayer that didn't address my question at all. In the depths of my heart, I began to think there wasn't an answer to my problem.
>
> After that, I kept quiet about my doubts and condemned myself for having them. The guiltier I felt, the less I prayed or served at church. Talking to God only made me feel worse.
>
> Even after I had completed my master's degree in psychology and was working as a therapist, I still felt that something was missing. I hadn't resolved the pain of my past. When I began having panic attacks, I saw a Christian therapist who helped me see that my ACDF background was affecting my personal, professional, and spiritual life.

In the safety of those sessions, and later in a church-related support group, I admitted that I doubted God. I remember telling the group that I felt like God's promises were empty and that they didn't apply to my dysfunctional family. Other people admitted the same struggles, and we cried together. I knew I wasn't alone. After that, I quit condemning myself, which helped me move ahead in my recovery. Through other people's love and acceptance, I understood God's grace on a deeper level. That opened up a new world of who I was in Christ.

We want God's love to free us of our doubts, but our pride as "looking-good Christians" wedges us into a corner. Our position is further reinforced by certain powerful undercurrents in today's communities of faith. These undercurrents, which we'll call *myths,* are identified in the following paragraphs. We've chosen to describe them in blunt, "bottom line" terms. The version of each myth that we usually hear from other Christians is much more subtle than the wording we use here, but just as damaging. Accepting the myths even in their subtle forms adds to that traffic jam between our minds and our hearts and makes it difficult for God's love to penetrate.

Myth: Becoming a Christian solves all our problems.
Fact: Becoming a Christian means salvation, but it doesn't exempt Christians from pain—even pain from the hurts of the past.

Many of us answered the altar call because we thought that Christianity was a magic potion that would solve our problems. We heard, "Jesus is the answer," so we thought we would "try" him. (This is typical of the "magical" thinking that ACDFs employ to solve problems. We can't find the answers, so we grab at anything.) When we found that God didn't make life easier for us and that we still felt depressed, we became disillusioned. We subconsciously viewed Christianity as one more thing that didn't work, and we may have even thought, *Not even God can help me.*

Those who buy into this myth imply that Christians who do have problems must have some hidden sin in their lives. Yet we know this isn't true, because God allows pain and suffering. The Old Testament prophet Jeremiah sank into the mud of a cistern at the hands of Judah's wicked rulers (Jer. 38:6). Paul endured his "thorn in the flesh" (2 Cor. 12:7–10). Jesus suffered to the fullest extent on the cross. Sometimes God provides a way out, but not always.

Myth: Christians have the victory over sin, so sin is a problem only for those with weak faith.

Fact: All Christians struggle with sin.

This myth tells us that we can overcome sin by praising the Lord, claiming the victory, and having an "attitude of gratitude." Christians who buy into this myth are uncomfortable around struggling people, including ACDFs working through recovery. These Christians urge us to move on as quickly as possible.

Even though God is the divine physician, he doesn't choose to heal everyone or alleviate all our struggles with sin. Some alcoholics are healed; for others, struggle is a necessary part of growth.

We see believers throughout the Bible struggling with sin. We find special comfort that the apostle Paul described his struggle as a "war" (Rom. 7:23) and agonized over it: ". . . I have the desire to do what is good, but I cannot carry it out. For what I do is not the good I want to do; no, the evil I do not want to do—this I keep on doing. Now if I do what I do not want to do, it is no longer I who do it, but it is sin living in me that does it" (Rom. 7:18–20).

This myth particularly damages those of us who are compulsive. Our compulsive nature seems like a lion that can never be tamed, but this myth suggests that it can be tamed by simply "claiming a victory." This only aggravates the problem or becomes an addiction of its own.

Myth: Christians should de-emphasize feelings.

Fact: We should experience the feelings God gave us and bring them to him, especially when we don't understand them.

Many Christians believe that feelings are to be disciplined, buffeted, or controlled if you want to truly follow God. Here are a few of Curt's experiences with this myth:

> When I was new in my faith, Christians told me, "Curt, ignore those feelings, and do what God wants you to do." I poured my heart out to one Christian, who simply thumped his Bible and said, "That's just a feeling. What does the Bible say?" He told me that listening to my feelings would get me into trouble. So I ignored my feelings, which wasn't difficult—I learned how to do this growing up.

God created feelings. He is a full-feeling Being, expressing anger (Jon. 4:1), hurt (Hos. 11:1–4), and joy (Neh. 8:10). Much of the Bible talks about feelings, especially in Old Testament poetry and prophecy. King David of the Old Testament, a "man after his [God's] own heart" (1 Sam. 13:14), struggled with feelings openly:

> My heart is in anguish within me;
>   the terrors of death assail me.
> Fear and trembling have beset me:
>   horror has overwhelmed me. . . .
> But I call to God,
>   and the Lord saves me.
> Evening, morning and noon I cry out in distress
>   and he hears my voice.
>   —Psalm 55:4, 5, 16, 17

David felt the full strength of his emotions and surrendered them to God. We can do the same thing.

Cutting off our feelings cuts off a part of who we are. It isolates our emotional lives from our faith and tempts us to lead two lives—a secular one and a spiritual one. How much wiser to deal with feelings, even the ugliest ones, through our faith.

Myth: Praying and reading the Bible are all you need to get better.

Fact: We also need the powerful tools of close fellowship and worship.

Jesus discipled the apostles by spending time with them, talking with them, asking questions, and even telling stories. Recovery, which can also be a form of discipleship, is not a solo trip. In support groups, we break the isolation, we hear others' experiences, we receive the love of others so that we can see God through them. This teaches us to trust people.

Worship is important, too. Through it, we relate to God as a powerful Creator who doesn't abandon us. It helps us express back to God the truths of the Scripture in a personal way.

Myth: Doing good works heals the hurts inside us because we are making the world a better place in which to live.

Fact: Burned-out servants who give of themselves for the wrong reasons harm themselves and others.

A selfless attitude does create good feelings, but these feelings can sour if we're serving to bolster a sense of inadequacy. We hope that our service will make us feel "good enough," but it doesn't, because no amount of service can make up for low self-esteem. Even small failures become "larger than life," and we burn out.

Jenny, a typical ACDF, found this out:

> I taught Sunday school for eight years. I loved it at first, but then some kids dropped out. When I got mar-

ried and had children, I didn't have time to prepare as I had before. I couldn't hold the kids' attention as well. I lost my "superteacher" identity.

I asked my pastor for a year off, but he persuaded me not to take it. He said I was the only one in the church who had the skill and ability to teach high-school kids. I loved and respected my pastor, so I continued. But the more I "did for God," the emptier I felt. I knew the kids could see through me, and I even thought about leaving the church.

Then I read a book about ACDFs and went into therapy. I saw how I was codependent, sacrificing myself for everyone else. I saw that others needed to help out instead of relying on me. I realized that I had gone through the motions of serving even when I didn't have time, because I had learned in my dysfunctional family that if I worked for God, he would love me.

I quit teaching Sunday school and took time to begin healing. My pastor eventually began to understand. Now he's asked me to start an ACDF group, and I'm thinking about it.

Myth: Just keep believing, and your doubts will fade.
Fact: Doubts (or "crises of faith") may gradually fade, but like anger and past hurt, they must be faced.

Service to others should be woven through our recovery, but it isn't a substitute for working through our ACDF issues. Our service doesn't truly help other people when our buried feelings are causing us to ooze with poor self-esteem. Hidden rage creates a "drivenness" that alienates people instead of helping them.

Since ACDFs have felt emotionally or physically abandoned by the people who were supposed to protect them, they may be plagued by doubts about God. They have questions rumbling just below the surface that they're not aware of until a calamity occurs.

These questions then surface: Is God there? Is he who he says he is? Is Scripture really true? Why is there a gap between what I read in the Bible ("God is love" [1 John 4:16]) and what I experience? Many of these doubts are subconscious, and we suppress them because they seem so wrong.

In gatherings of ACDFs who are Christians, it's not uncommon to hear these comments:

> "All these years I've been acting like I believe what other Christians believe, but I'm not sure that I do."
>
> "I told my support group that I'm not sure I can trust God. I don't experience the promises of the Bible."

Don't expect most church circles to feel comfortable with these doubts. Sometimes these comments may even evoke verbal attacks and shame. Yet we can't bury our doubts. We each need to find a person or group that will listen to us express our crises of faith and help us work through them.

Myth: Guilt is good.

Fact: Appropriate guilt spurs our consciences; inappropriate guilt cripples us.

When healthy people hear sermons about spiritual behaviors that they haven't been practicing, they feel "healthy guilt." They brush themselves off and ask God to help them do better.

ACDFs generally overdo guilt. We ask forgiveness, but we never feel forgiven. When we read Scripture with the healthier eyes of recovery, we discover that Bible heroes were ordinary people who sinned but whom God worked through to accomplish great things. Most of them could be disqualified as leaders for today's churches—Noah for drunkenness, David for adultery, the apostle Paul for murder. It was this murderer himself who wrote, "There is now no condemnation for those who are in Christ Jesus"

(Rom. 8:1). We have access to God's forgiveness and grace; it is foolish and even wrong to reject these gifts from God.

Another problem is that most of us heap on ourselves inappropriate false guilt that we learned in our dysfunctional families. We judge ourselves harshly and take ourselves too seriously. If we don't follow the letter of the law, we feel inadequate. We condemn ourselves in the same ways in which we were condemned in the past. It was wrong when others did this to us as children. It's wrong when we do it to ourselves.

As recovering ACDFs, we no longer allow the inappropriate guilt and shame of our past to rule us. We look to a loving Father who wants to know us and be involved in our lives.

Religious Shame

The myths just described typify a general attitude of religious shame among some Christians. It's as if someone decided long ago that guilt was a good way to get us to try harder.

A religious-shame mentality views all of life through smoked glass: having fun is bad, having problems is bad, being a sexual person is bad, being ill is bad, being too rich is bad, being too poor is bad. It promotes unwritten rules such as these:

- Strong people don't cry.
- Spiritual people are always in control.
- Wise people don't ask questions.

In reality, the opposite of these is true. People are stronger when they cry; they're more spiritual when they relinquish control to God; it takes wisdom to see fallacies and possible consequences.

Shame is different from appropriate guilt. With guilt, we feel that we did something wrong, but with shame we feel that we are wrong to the core. We are damaged goods. This kind of shame grows out of shame-based childhood experiences, not guilt over recent sin.

If we forget the common distorted views of a blaming and shaming God, we see God as a loving Father full of grace. When the father spied the prodigal son down the road, he ran out to meet him (Luke 15:20–24). The father didn't say, "You blew it. Shame on you." He threw a party instead. That's the picture of God that we as ACDFs need to understand and remember. That's also a picture of the response we need from fellow Christians.

You may be wondering . . .

Q *If I'm a "new creation" in Christ (2 Cor. 5:17), doesn't that mean I have overcome sin?*

A Christ purchased our redemption and position in heaven, and we now have the power of the Holy Spirit to equip us (John 14:17; 16:13, 15). Yet this doesn't take away our sin nature, and it doesn't cancel the handicap of the dysfunctional family.

Battling one's sin nature is not a sign of weak faith. Even strong Christians battle their sin natures. The Early Church, which included many who had walked with Jesus and had received the Holy Spirit at Pentecost, struggled in "much discussion" over the sin of racial prejudice (Acts 15:7).

Q *Why do some ACDFs go overboard in expressing feelings?*

A Those repressed feelings have been trapped behind a dam for years, and in recovery, the dam bursts. We are so inexperienced at expressing feelings that we sometimes do so in less-than-tactful ways. That's why some therapists ask clients to write down exact wording if they want to confront someone. Seeing the words on paper gives ACDFs a change to consider the impact of their words and rethink what they're going to say.

This isn't to say that we should "live in our feelings," doing whatever they dictate. We listen to our feelings, face whatever truth they may be telling us, and discard untruths.

CHAPTER 10

"Compulsive? Who Me?"

"I'll never act like my mother!"

"I'll never be out of control like my dad was."

We have mumbled these classic ACDF statements under our breath in disgust; we have screamed them in rage; we have groaned them in prayer. We vowed that we would be different, yet as adults, we find ourselves turning to addictive behaviors just as one or both of our parents did.

It's as if we think, *Dad wore a blue suit, and he was an alcoholic* (or a perfectionist or overeater), *so I'll wear a brown one and be different from him.* Yet no matter how many days we get up and put on that brown suit, we find that by sundown we're wearing the blue one again.

We may fool ourselves for a while by acquiring the education, friends, or job success than our compulsive parent did not have. We may even excuse ourselves by thinking that our compulsion is not as "crazy" as that parent's was: *Dad was an alcoholic, but I'm simply a "workaholic."* Yet inside we are the same. We experience the same inner fear or hopelessness or anger our compulsive parent felt. We confuse and alienate the people around us just as our compulsive parent did.

We live out what we learned at home: to use compulsive behavior to manage inner pain.

Here's Tom's story. He tells the various ways he managed his pain.

> When I was a freshman in high school, my parents gave me three pairs of polyester bell-bottom pants. One pair was green, another was brown, and the other was

navy blue. They were all too short. When I asked if I could have some Levis, my mom said, "You have the most beautiful pants. Why don't you wear them?"

My mom was a powerful woman, and I couldn't make her understand. I felt guilty because I was the minister's son but I still wanted to look like my friends at school. I couldn't bear to wear the polyester pants, so I always wore the other two pairs of pants I owned. Then my friends teased me about wearing those same pants all the time. Still, it was better than wearing those "flood pants."

About that same time, I developed an addiction to lust. I couldn't get hold of pornography, so I searched the women's magazines for scantily clad women. I felt so guilty, that I practiced a self-torturing type of masturbation ritual. That didn't ease the guilt or pain. At thirteen, I molested a two-year-old.

My dad talked to a psychologist and told me, "Your sister had a similar incident once." Then he dropped it.

At sixteen, I began practicing bulimia. I would eat three plates of food, throw up, and then eat dessert. I ran over fifty miles a week. My entire family was overweight, and I didn't want to be like them.

After ten years of this, I saw that I was destroying my body, so I tried to channel this frenzy into workaholism. I quit throwing up, but I still felt inadequate. I had become a counselor, hoping to find meaning in helping others. I didn't feel I was helping them as much as I thought I should, so I decreased my client load.

As I talked with my wife about my depression, I began to realize how hurt I was by my childhood. I'd never realized that I had been using all these addictions to "numb out" and to forget my past. In therapy and support groups, I began to look at childhood feelings and let go of them. I saw how I had copied my parents' addictions with food and work. My parents have always craved sweets, and they can't relax. On holidays, it wasn't unusual for them to have Monopoly tournaments that lasted fifteen hours!

I am still attending a Twelve-Step group for sexual addiction, and I'm learning to deal with my feelings rather than retreating into lust. Both my career and my marriage are beginning to blossom. I'm learning that I don't have to please other people. I can be me—and people might even like me better for it.

Tom portrays the ACDF's search for pain management. He used sex, food, and work, but they didn't alleviate his pain. Like many Christians, he skipped the best-known "painkillers"—alcoholism and drug addiction. His life shows that bulimia, pornography, and self-abuse can be addictions as well. Psychologists are learning that people can become addicted to almost any substance or behavior, such as gambling, sex, overeating, overexercising, nicotine, caffeine, shopping or spending money, religion, relationships, and watching television.

Many compulsions seem so innocent. Mom reads romance novels to fill the emptiness in her life. Dad builds furniture or works on the car because he doesn't want to be with the family to talk about feelings.

We know that a substance or behavior has become addictive when it follows what is commonly called the *addictive cycle:*

Preoccupation: We think about it; we look forward to it.

Ritualization: We prepare for it by thinking, *I'll wait until everyone leaves the house, and then . . . or I'll need this* [a drug, food, and so on] *later when I. . . .*

Compulsive Behavior: We act out the obsession.

Guilt: We feel guilty that we acted out. To relieve these bad feelings, we turn to *preoccupation.*

You may be asking, What's the difference between an addiction and a compulsion? In the past, *addiction* was used to describe dependencies that affected the body chemically, such as drugs and alcohol. *Compulsions* were thought to be behavioral only. Now it's understood that decisions that are made over and over form a chemical path on the neurotransmitters in the brain. These paths make it likely that the behavior will be repeated. So, technically speaking, compulsions are chemical also, and the distinction is gone.

As we look at several common addictions, we'll use the words *addiction* and *compulsion* according to their popular definitions.

Chemical Addiction

Studies have shown that four times as many ACAs become substance abusers as non-ACAs.[1] While researchers look for genetic links, the behavior link is obvious: alcoholic parents set an example of turning to a substance to fill unmet needs.

Alcohol. The problem of alcoholism is not limited to drunks lying in the street. Many professionals are "weekend drinkers," who refuse to miss a Friday-night binge. "Dry drunks" no longer drink, but their impatient, argumentative behavior remains unchanged. They often pick up other compulsions to fill the void that quitting alcohol has left.

Nicotine, sugar, and caffeine. These substances are technically drugs because they alter the structure or function of the body when used. They produce a physical "high" and "low" in most people. They become a compulsion when they're used regularly to manage pain, to energize, or to relax.

Prescription drugs. The most common kind of drug abuse in the church involves the overuse of tranquilizers, sedatives (barbiturates), stimulants (amphetamines, methamphetamines), and pain-killing drugs. At first, we may use these drugs to stay awake, to go to sleep, or to curb our appetites, but they become habit-forming. Doctors sometimes prescribe these drugs indiscriminately, or patients will go to several doctors at the same time to get them. It's easy for us to fool ourselves, because prescription drug abuse doesn't seem illegal.

Illegal drug use. Baby-boomers who smoked marijuana as hippies in the sixties now wear business suits and relax at home with the same habit. One woman lamented in this way about her husband:

> I'm trying to get my husband more interested in church. He finally came with me, and we met a couple he liked. We had them over, and what do you know? He and the other husband both smoke marijuana. The other wife and I felt sick. Instead of helping each other, these men were comparing favorite pipes and special blends. Even church people do drugs.

ACDFs who filled the "acting-out child" role in their families are most likely to use cocaine, hallucinogens (LSD and the like), and narcotics (such as heroin, morphine, and codeine) to manage their pain. Those who used these drugs as teens often quit and switch to a supposedly more grown-up compulsion, such as workaholism.

Toxic inhalants. Common household substances, when abused, produce not only intoxication but also hallucinations and serious body damage. These substances include paint thinner, gasoline, airplane glue, lighter fluid, and other vapor-producing chemicals. At first, this problem occurred more frequently with children and adolescents, but now adults use this addiction as well.

Sexual Addiction

According to psychologist Dr. Patrick Carnes, there are three levels of sexual addiction:[2]

Level One: compulsive masturbation, repeated promiscuous relationships (heterosexual and homosexual), pornography and strip shows, and prostitution.
Level Two: exhibitionism, voyeurism, indecent calls, and liberties.
Level Three: molestation, incest, rape, and sexual violence.

Exhibitionism can be something as common as pulling down one's pants and bending over (called *mooning*). *Repeated promiscuous relationships* are euphemistically called *cruising* or *hustling.*

Many sex addicts are now figuring out that they were sexually abused as children. In their loneliness and alienation, they are reliving those experiences. The good news is that more counselors and literature now deal with sexual addiction.

Food Addictions

Some have called overeating the "Christian sin." Between potluck dinners, fund-raising events, and ice cream socials, it's difficult to avoid it.

Compulsive overeating and dieting. This means using food as a soothing agent, just as alcoholics use alcohol. Compulsive overeaters give a lot of time and thought to food. They look forward to eating, especially when they're alone. They may eat a salad when they meet a friend for lunch, but after they bid the friend good-bye, they load up on ice cream. As the compulsion progresses, diets quit working.

Since magazines, movies, and television tell us that to be thin is to be attractive, many overeaters feel driven to lose weight. This creates a "yo-yo" cycle in which the person repeatedly diets for a few months and then overeats again. This cycle creates a desperation that often leads to eating disorders.

Eating disorders. *Bulimics* binge, usually on "forbidden foods," and then purge themselves by vomiting, overexercising, or taking laxatives. *Anorexics*—those who ease their pain by starving themselves—get high from feelings of starvation and control. They usually see themselves as fat, no matter how thin they are.

Many people assume that only adolescent women are bulimic or anorexic, but this isn't true. Men and women of all ages use these disorders to control their weight, and to control their lives. Men who have to stay a certain weight for their athletic careers are especially prone.

Work Addiction

"Workaholism" is not the love of hard work; it's working compulsively for reasons that have little to do with work. People get hooked on productivity because they need to be needed, they need to control, or they need to feel that they accomplished something in order to feel worthwhile.

Workaholism is also a "Christian sin," especially if it's church work. Tom's parents were "busyness addicts." His dad was a minister and worked eighty hours a week to be exactly what his congregation wanted.

Time flies when you engage in your compulsion. Even though Tom's dad worked long hours, it was never enough. He found that he always worked longer than he had expected to, so he began promising his wife that he would be home by 10:00 P.M., but he never was. Even though he knew he was placing stress on his family, he kept doing it.

Some workaholics are perfectionists, too. They can't relax, and they can't tolerate failure. They are driven by a desire to be "good enough," and their short-lived victories are their "highs."

Religious Addiction

All faiths have religious addicts, but let's examine some of the ways that this addiction manifests itself in Christian circles.

Hooked on "highs." Those seeking religious "highs" look for newer, better, more exciting experiences to help them maintain or recapture emotional "highs." To create this fervor, they may spend all their spare time attending church activities, reading favorite Bible passages, or watching religious television programs. Since religious "highs" satisfy the emotions but not the inner spirit, it takes more and more of this frenzied activity to maintain a "high" until the person "crashes."

Hooked on rigidity. Many perfectionistic religious addicts grew up in strict authoritarian homes where there was no give and take. As children, they wanted to fly kites or build forts, but their parents didn't consider those activities spiritual, so they weren't allowed.

Now, as adults, they carry doctrine and practices to extremes. Every area of life becomes black or white. They feel guilty even about activities that their intellects say aren't wrong. They beat themselves up if they enjoy listening to soft rock music because they've been taught that it's bad. They maintain a facade of perfection and don't dare admit their fear, guilt, and anger.

These people can't afford to leave any work to the Holy Spirit, so they control their children's spiritual lives by insisting on certain practices. They refuse to listen to their teenagers' typical "crises of faith" questions, such as, How can I be sure that God exists?

Hooked on church workaholism. "Churchaholics" are involved with church as many days of the week as possible. Outside the church, they lose their niche and also their identity. As they move deeper into their compulsion, they distance themselves from friends, relatives, and spouses who don't involve themselves in church. They've always wanted to be "good enough," and church workaholism has shown them how.

Hooked on a leader. This type of religious addict feels the continued need to consult a "spiritual leader," who may motivate followers with the fear of hell and threats of losing salvation.

This extreme loyalty occurs because addicts of this sort want leaders to replace their dysfunctional parents. ACDFs from authoritarian families feel comfortable with such leaders because they are used to being told what to do. ACDFs from weak families can become devoted to leaders as if they've finally found the strength that was lacking in their dysfunctional parents.

Religious addicts are often hiding alcoholics in their family closets, and the hyperreligiosity of these addicts is a reaction to their relatives' uncontrolled behavior. They deny the pain that their families experienced, and they "stuff it" with religion.

None of this is to say that all Christians who go to church, read their Bibles, and pray several times a day are addicted. Someone has said, "You can never get too much of God," and in a sense this is true. The problem is that religious addicts don't seek God; they seek emotional highs, self-righteousness, control, or being controlled. Christians who are truly devoted to God rely on him as the author of wholeness, instead of themselves and their activities.

Which Recovery Comes First?

Dealing with ACDF issues doesn't cure compulsive behavior. The popular idea used to be that, if you dealt with underlying issues, compulsions would go away. That idea hasn't proved true. Instead, physical recovery from a compulsion is necessary to have enough clarity to deal with underlying ACDF issues. If our brains are dulled with alcohol or sugar, or preoccupied with pornography or lengthy "to do" lists, they won't work clearly. We need uncluttered minds to face our problems. Alan discovered this the hard way:

> I had had fifteen days of sobriety in AA when I attended my first ACDF meeting. I liked the honesty I found there, but I couldn't handle it. I started remembering how crazy my dad had acted and how my codependent mother had leaned on me for comfort. I couldn't resolve one thing before another came up. I was so new to sobriety that I couldn't stand all that emotional pain. I did what I had been doing for twenty years—I went drinking. Then I felt better.
>
> I then crawled back to AA and focused on my recovery from alcoholism. After a year of alcohol recovery, I returned to the ACDF meeting, and I began to understand my behavior better.

We recommend that ACDFs have six months to a year of recovery from their addictions before they dive into ACDF issues. This gives them time to learn how to handle their hurts without using the addictive behaviors. It also builds a foundation of surrender and forgiveness so essential to ACDF recovery.

Addiction Recovery

This one chapter can't possibly address the subject of addiction recovery adequately, but here are some guidelines to get you started.

Am I compulsive?   Not everyone who drinks alcohol is an alcoholic, nor is every overweight person a compulsive overeater. The following questions may help us determine if our behavior is compulsive:

- Does this activity give me a false sense of comfort, pride, or power?
- Is this activity harming me? Do I harm others because of this activity?
- Does this activity follow the addictive cycle—preoccupation, ritualization, acting out, guilt?

"Yes" answers mean that we rely on a behavior that is damaging ourselves and others. It may help to ask family members or close friends how they would answer these questions for us.

Treatment.   The obvious, but shortsighted, solution is to simply stop these behaviors. A few people with compulsive behaviors do succeed through steel-nerved self-control, but this route forces most of us to bury pain instead of facing it. It also increases false images of personal strength, which sets us up for more failure.

The best methods for treatment involve other people. Many compulsive people recover simply with the help of support groups (such as Twelve-Step groups); others need therapy as well; still others require a ten-day, thirty-day or sixty-day stay in a treatment center, with support-group assistance afterward.

"Addiction hopping." Since the ACDF tendencies make us so ripe for addictions, we need to be continually careful that we don't acquire new addictions, especially those that

already exist in our families. Even though we say we won't wear our parents' "blue suit" of alcoholism or workaholism, that blue suit is the model for handling anger and stress that we witnessed for years.

A potentially addictive behavior is the most attractive when we feel worthless. When we have problems with our marriages, our friends, or our jobs, we are tempted to repress anger. Going to an addiction-related support group at the first sign of preoccupation can save us a lot of potential pain. There we can share our pain and anger, and we can receive the encouragement of others who are fighting that addiction.

You may be wondering . . .

Q *If I have alcoholic parents, does that mean I'm going to be an alcoholic too?*

A Certain influences are working against you to encourage addictive behavior. You have watched your parents manage their pain through drinking, and most of us imitate our parents' behaviors whether we want to or not. Also, studies show that some people have a genetic predisposition to alcoholism, meaning that their genes are set up so that they are more likely to crave alcohol. You may be one of them.

Having alcoholic parents doesn't mean you have to become an alcoholic, though. It may mean that your satiation level is higher—that it takes more alcohol to get you drunk, or that you want to drink until you're drunk. The safest path is to abstain from drinking, but if you do drink, watch it carefully.

None of this means that you are doomed to become an alcoholic. Even with a predisposition, you still have a personal responsibility to take care of yourself. It may explain how some ACAs become alcoholics, but it doesn't mean they can't recover. We always have a choice.

Q   *Can I become addicted to ACDF recovery?*

A   Yes, but you don't have to. The key word is *balance*. A person with a family will find it difficult to attend ACDF meetings every day. Many of us would like to quit our jobs to focus on our recovery, but that isn't possible. So we go to as many support-group meetings as we can, and we try to balance recovery with other responsibilities.

Some families may accuse us of being "addicted to recovery," because it takes so much of our time. It's wise to explain our needs and how much our recovery is helping us. Explain that recovery won't take this much time forever, but for now, we do need time to read, to talk, and to attend meetings.

The Processes
of Our Recovery

CHAPTER 11

How Soon
Will This Be Over?

Recovery can be one of the best things that ever happens to you—and one of the worst things to experience. It makes our lives healthier and happier than ever before, but it's a painful valley to walk through. We wipe the smoked glass clean, but it takes a while, and our muscles ache from it.

A question frequently asked is, How long will recovery take?

Although recovery is a lifelong process, it takes two to three years to integrate healthier attitudes and skills into our lives. If we have addictions, we can usually add at least six months for recovery from each addiction.

Here's a road map of four phases of ACDF recovery:
Stop: Getting our attention
Look: Recognizing and accepting our problems
Listen: Recalling painful memories
Go: Integrating recovery into our lifestyles

These phases of recovery don't begin and end as if they were a road from point A to point B. Recovery is an upward spiral. We move through each phase many times, with different issues and a keener awareness.

STOP: Getting Our Attention
"Something is wrong."

The pain and anger of our dysfunctional childhoods that we've stored in the holding tanks of our subconscious

minds escape in different ways. For some of us, it's a slow
leak or a nagging itch. We fight more than usual with family members, or we develop phobias or sexual dysfunc-
tions. We can't concentrate, and we don't know why we're
so unhappy with life. We no longer care about God or the
things of God, and that worries us.

With others of us, the tank explodes. We are hit by surprise with divorce, loss of a job, death of a spouse, or a
stage-of-life crisis. Suddenly we feel a great deal of pain.
We say to ourselves, *Uh-oh, this one's too big to fix.* We can't
hold back the pain. Here are some of the more common
ways that the holding tank explodes:

"Frozen rage."   We become extremely angry that our
parents weren't emotionally available to us. The anger
seethes within us, and there seems to be no resolution to it.
Sometimes we turn this anger inward, and we become
deeply depressed.

Illness.   Eighty percent of all illnesses are stress-
related.[1] Stress thrashes the body with allergies, asthma,
skin rashes, arthritis, cancer, infections, temporomandib-
ular joint disorders (TMJ), immune-system diseases, and
collagen diseases such as lupus. Even supposedly simple
problems such as headaches, constipation, diarrhea, muscle tension, and sleep disorders may mean that something
is wrong inside us.

Some medical doctors now give their patients question-
naires about family background. When they suspect that
patients' illnesses are connected to dysfunctional family issues, they recommend support groups or therapy. One
common example of this is the treatment of anorexia. Doctors recommend support groups and therapy because
medical treatment alone does not help.

Post-traumatic stress disorder (PTSD). This problem became better known when Vietnam War veterans had re-

curring flashbacks of gruesome battlefield experiences. They remembered vividly the sights, sounds, and smells of battle not only as they dreamed but also while they were awake.

Some ACDFs experience PTSD as they recall traumatic childhood events that they repressed long ago. They tried to forget the "wars" of their childhood, but the pain remained. PTSD is often accompanied by panic attacks.

Panic attacks. During panic attacks, people suffer from heart palpitations, shortness of breath, dizziness, sweating, or vomiting. Thoughts fly through their heads faster than they can handle them. For example, agoraphobics (those with a fear of not being able to get back to a secure place) often experience panic attacks in open spaces, especially in crowded ones.

Panic attacks are a physical response to pain that we are no longer able to repress. It's difficult to figure out what present-day circumstances trigger an attack, because they resemble events and feelings from childhood that we have buried. As adults, we react to these similar situations by feeling abandoned, angry, or out of control, but we don't know why. We replay the pain and helplessness that we felt as children.

Tad tells his story:

> I was about to enter a prestigious graduate school to fulfill what I thought was God's will for my life. One night, while talking to a friend, I felt my heart begin to pound. My mind raced as if I were on some kind of drug that had slammed me into hyperspace. My body felt squashed, my face got tight, and my hands shook. I tried to walk outside because I was sweating so much. I thought I was dying or going crazy. Was this an out-of-the-body experience? Would it ever end?
>
> It did end, only for others to occur—usually when I was going through something painful with a girlfriend or with my job. I struggled to understand what was hap-

pening to me. I was trying to live a good life: I went to church, sang in the choir, taught Bible studies, read my Bible, and prayed regularly.

The doctor said they were panic attacks. At first, I denied that they had happened. I was afraid to tell Christian people about them because I thought they would say I had mental problems.

Then I tried to spiritualize them away. I figured I had some terrible sin in my life, so I asked forgiveness. I listened to Christian radio programs all the time so that I could be more spiritual. I followed people's advice to "claim the victory."

I felt completely alone. It seemed that no one, including God, could reach inside me and calm the craziness there. I had no answers, only questions, and I was giving up hope that I would regain control again. I went through three years of soul searching—tears, fear, prayer, suicidal thoughts, failed relationships, and advice from well-meaning friends.

I ended up in the counseling office with a perceptive Christian therapist who was himself an ACDF. I told my story. There I found out that having grown up in a dysfunctional family had set patterns and feelings into motion that I had not been aware of.

As I went to counseling and to support groups, I didn't feel so alone. I faced the pain of having been raised in a dysfunctional family. I talked about my problems with my parents, expressed my anger, and learned better ways of dealing with life. I felt relieved. The attacks didn't mean I was crazy. They represented old problems that needed attention.

During my attacks, I began to reach out to others instead of isolating myself. Sometimes I called other people on the telephone and talked as well as I could. As painful as the attacks were, I eventually began to sense that God loved me. He was allowing my pain to come out of my subconscious mind. I trusted that he knew what I was ready to remember.

Even though I'm in recovery, these attacks still occur at times. I see them as warnings that I feel isolated and that I need to talk about a problem. They show me that I'm once again trying to be too many things to too many people.

What to Expect from This Phase

There's often a rush of feelings at the beginning of recovery. Some of us are euphoric as we reveal all that we've kept hidden for years. It's a relief to discover that we're not crazy, that we're only handicapped by dysfunctionality.

Others of us feel depressed, even suicidal. The pain of our past is too great, and we would rather die. It helps to remember that suicidal feelings are not uncommon and that they are different from suicidal intentions. Suicidal feelings are usually a strong desire to escape, while suicidal intentions mean that the person has the suicide planned in detail and does not intend to seek help.

If you have suicidal intentions or severe suicidal feelings, seek professional help immediately. Call a suicide hot line, and find out about local counseling centers or outpatient county facilities. Keep in touch with people.

If outpatient treatment doesn't help, don't be afraid to be hospitalized. Only a small percentage of ACDFs in recovery need hospitalization, and they need it only temporarily to manage a life crisis. After the crisis subsides, they usually find that outpatient treatment and support groups meet their needs.

> **LOOK:** Recognizing and Accepting the Problem
> "I grew up in a dysfunctional home."

Those of us who are ACDFs from Christian families don't like to admit that our upbringing wasn't healthy.

Christians are supposed to be nothing less than victorious creatures in Christ. We think our faith magically exempts us from problems and that growing up in a pastor's family exempts us doubly from them! For some of us, it's easier to admit that we have a compulsion than to admit that our families were dysfunctional. *True, I may have a "little problem" with overeating,* we think, *but don't pick on my parents. My family life was wonderful!* That desire to protect the family and its secrets dies hard.

What to Do

Acquaint yourself with the issues. The "softest" approach to learning about ACDF issues is to read books on the subject. Literature is helpful in the beginning because you don't have to admit anything to anybody; you can even sneak the book home in a brown paper bag if you like. Reading is convenient, and you can gobble up the book or digest it slowly. Attending support groups or therapy feels riskier in the beginning, but it also helps us understand the issues quickly.

Identify with the experiences of others. What good is it to hear other people's experiences? Their stories ring bells for us like nothing else. They bring up old memories, with the realization, *My parents did the same thing. So that's why I'm this way.* This identification helps us come out of denial and see how much our families affected us. We hear these stories in support groups, group therapy, and the coffeeshop communion that often occurs after these meetings.

Tell your own story. Some ACDFs may shrink from talking about themselves for a while, or they may talk but mention insignificant things only. Still others are eager to open up immediately.

Telling our stories is valuable because it means we're

coming out of denial. We talk out loud about the parts of ourselves that we've kept hidden. We reveal the child within to the outside world, and we find out that this child can be accepted.

What to Expect from This Phase

Unless our parents and siblings are also in recovery, they may resent our exposing the family secrets. If the dysfunctionality was nonchemical, it will be particularly hard for them to understand, because the family seemed so "normal." Like Donna, we may not tell our parents that we're going to meetings. Even pastors and Christian friends may not want to hear about our recovery experiences.

If you speak up, don't be surprised by reactions such as these:

"You're not trusting God enough. Just let go of it."

"Everybody's got problems. You don't need to go to that group."

"Isn't this something that psychologists made up for wimps who can't get through life? Why do you keep whining?"

"That's fine for you, but I don't need that."

When you get comments like these, explanations don't usually help. You simply admit that you have a problem, and that you're dealing with it. If the people who make these comments are Christians, ask them to pray for you. Not only will they be helping you, but they will be giving God an opportunity to speak to them about your recovery.

Negative feedback can hurt, but we don't have to feel isolated. Many of us find that a support group becomes like a family to us, giving us the validation we need in recovery.

LISTEN: Getting in Touch With
Painful Memories
"I'm remembering things I forgot long ago."

We "protected" ourselves by denying and trying to forget painful childhood experiences, but that only embedded them deeper within us.

Comments in support groups often trigger memories. The memories may begin with feelings of fear or anger, and it may take a while to recall the exact event.

We recall these memories sporadically. Sometimes no hidden memories will surface for six months, and then we will remember four painful childhood incidents in one week. We trust that the Lord knows the best timing for us to remember the pain we buried.

Some of these incidents may not seem like much, and they wouldn't be, except that they keep replaying themselves in our lives. Here's a simple event that replays itself in James's life:

> When I was seven, I brought home a lot of math homework on Halloween night. My father wouldn't let me go out until I had done the homework. I guessed at the answers so that I could finish quickly.
>
> But my father checked it and accused me of guessing. "You don't know the answers at all," he pounded away at me. "You're guessing! Three! Five! Twenty-six! You don't know! You need to know the answers. How come you don't know the answers?"
>
> I see now that my dad was frustrated, and I was scared because I didn't want to disappoint him. To this day, I shut down if someone hovers over me. I freeze because I'm afraid they'll see that I'm stupid.
>
> Recently a professor stood behind me as I worked on an experiment. I could hear my father talking when

the professor said, "Show me how you're going to do this experiment."

I couldn't move until the professor had left. For a few minutes, the world stopped, and I felt as if I were seven again. When he went on to the next student, I started breathing again.

Feelings of inadequacy replayed themselves many times in James's life, but he had never understood why. Recalling the incident with his father and others like it helped him in his recovery because he saw how these incidents had convinced him that he was inadequate, nervous, and even stupid. Now, as an adult, he sees that he wasn't stupid at all, but that he was a normal kid who had raced through his homework so that he could go out and collect candy.

As memories surface, we need to talk about them. That authenticates them. At first, James wasn't sure why the incident with the professor had bothered him so much, but as he talked about it in his support group, he remembered the childhood incident. Others in the group identified with it, and this helped him know he wasn't alone.

GO: Integrating Recovery into Our Life-styles
"I'm learning what normal behavior is."

We use what we learn in order to adopt healthier behavior patterns toward ourselves, toward others, and toward God.

Accept yourself. We "love" ourselves in the *agape* sense, meaning that we do what is best, or healthy, for ourselves. We also show mercy to ourselves as we would to any other person. Much of this comes from understanding that we are valued by God and that he doesn't discount us because of the "crazy" ways that we have behaved.

We respect ourselves, too. We avoid codependent tendencies by not volunteering too much and by not getting involved with people who need too much from us. As we learn to maintain healthy boundaries, we don't subject ourselves to unhealthy people who run us down.

We even learn to be assertive. We speak up for ourselves even when it may be difficult for others to listen, especially when we're accused, pushed, or belittled. We become familiar with phrases like these:

> "I disagree. I don't think what you're saying about me is true."
>
> "Thanks for your suggestions, but I'm not going to push myself that much."
>
> "I don't think that would be something that would help me."

Perhaps the most difficult task in self-acceptance is to no longer look for approval and affirmation from others. Instead, we seek God's approval and direction from what we sense that he's communicating to us. We trust ourselves to know God and to listen to him.

Pursue serenity.   As we accept ourselves and get to know God as a generous, loving parent, we find tranquillity and wholeness. We gradually shed the tension, hostility, and panic that have characterized our lives.

Our confidence grows as we get to know God's true character through a more honest prayer life, through worship, and through support-group discussions. We no longer feel as insecure in God's love, and it finally seems that there is hope for the future.

Since we no longer let the past cloud the present, we can make better decisions. We weigh alternatives and consequences without letting others push us into wrong choices. We consult advisers but not every single friend.

Attach to others in healthy ways.   We break out of our prisons of alienation and form close bonds with others. We no longer assume that people will abandon us, although we realize that they will disappoint us if we put expectations on them that are too high. We reserve loyalty for those who earn it.

One of the ways we know that God loves us is by the way others in support groups know and love us. We receive this healthy love in the following ways:

- We accept compliments and appreciation.
- We do not withdraw when others want to serve us or do us favors.
- We risk ourselves enough to share our needs with others.

Recovery Tools To Consider

Reading recovery books and going to support groups are essential for recovery. We find people in those groups with whom we can connect, and we spend time together outside of our groups.

Those who are transparent about feelings and who have reliable support systems may work through recovery with only those tools. However, if we find ourselves dealing with excessive anger and repressed trauma (especially repressed memories of sexual abuse), we may need professional help as well.

Therapy provides the one-on-one attention that many of us never received while growing up. It's a chance to receive the full attention of someone else, a change to be "completely heard." For those of us who went through childhood in isolation, this is the chance to bond with someone. For those of us who have never trusted anyone, we know that in our therapists we each have someone who is legally bound to confidentiality.

Therapists are trained to create a safe environment for the child within to question, to weep, or to get angry. They can also help us monitor and manage rage in a crisis, and they may give us specific suggestions for handling this rage. Therapists can also help in a crisis because they recognize physical disorders, deep psychological hurt, or true suicidal intentions. Many of us find that investing the time and money in therapy makes us more accountable and keeps us from denying that we have problems.

With or without professional help, God can help us do the important work of reparenting the child within. This listening, protecting, and re-teaching of the child within spans the last three phases of recovery and becomes a major part of it. Our next chapter shows how to do that.

You may be wondering . . .

Q *How do I choose a therapist?*
A Get recommendations from friends, support-group members, and counseling centers at churches. You may want to see what your health insurance covers.

It's usually best to choose a therapist who is a committed Christian and who is supportive of and preferably involved in a Twelve-Step program. If you are satisfied with the therapist's licenses or credentials, ask for a consultation.

Most people prefer a therapist that they "click with." See if you feel comfortable with the therapist's personality, age, gender, marital status, denominational preference, and the degree of comfort or confrontation that he or she uses. When we are working through the pain of a particular trauma, such as abuse, we may prefer therapists who have worked through the same issues.

Gender is important to many. If you want to work out problems with your father, it may help to see a male therapist. However, you may not be ready to do this if you were abused by your father, in which case a female therapist is better.

Some ACDFs never find a suitable therapist because the process is so scary for them. They're not ready to settle down and work out problems.

Going to a therapist isn't a replacement for going to a support group. Both are helpful to recovery.

CHAPTER 12

Reparenting the Child Within

Our task in recovery is to be the parents to ourselves that our own parents were unable to be. Many of us raised ourselves, using a lot of guesswork and molding ourselves after a television hero or an older kid down the street.

Now we have the opportunity to reparent ourselves. It isn't easy, but it's possible. Here are some steps to follow.

1. Awaken Your Child Within.

Many of us have shut the door on our childhood and don't want to think about it, much less recall any details. Yet inside our childhood memories lies the trapped child-like child within that we have abandoned.

We underestimate the importance of our child within, who was so humble, teachable, and trusting at one time. Those childlike characteristics were the ones that Jesus said would make a person the "greatest in the kingdom of heaven" (Matt. 18:4).

One way to awaken this child within is to watch how children play. If you don't have access to children, go to a park and watch how simple, teachable, and trusting they are.

We discover the child within ourselves by recalling our own childhood. What is your earliest positive memory? Your earliest negative one? Did you have a pet? What sounds do you remember?

Look at pictures of yourself as a child. What expression is on your face? Were you a happy child? What does it look like you were thinking? What did you like to do as a child? Were you a bubble blower? A fort builder?

It's important not to try to recall our childhoods in isolation. Show those childhood pictures to others, and tell them what you were like. They may identify with you and offer some sorely lacking affirmation and love for that child within. If your childhood was particularly painful, you may need a therapist to help you manage the fears that come with doing this.

As we value the child within, we regenerate this teachable, trusting part of ourselves that was stamped out. We find some of the best parts of ourselves that have been missing for a long time.

2. Listen to That Child's Messages.

Legitimate needs. The childlike child within sends us messages of neediness that we often ignore. In recovery, we no longer dismiss what the child within says when we're upset; we listen to the needs expressed.

We understand that when feelings come over us as we make decisions, the child within is communicating something. We wait for memories about those feelings, and we understand that this process keeps us from making poor decisions or overreacting to nonthreatening situations later.

Here's how Kerry listens to her child within:

> I was supposed to go to a committee meeting one time, but it seemed as if my child within didn't want to go. Part of me thought, *Go anyway. You're supposed to.*
>
> So I let that child within wail away for a minute: *Those meetings aren't helping anybody!*
>
> I asked myself if this were true. *Are these meetings unfruitful? Have I, once again, sold myself to a lost cause?* I thought about the meetings and decided they did some good.

But still, I knew my child within must have been reluctant for some reason. Maybe I didn't want to go because I was exhausted and needed rest. I knew this was a possibility, because I often do that. So I figured out how I could come home from work early and rest before the meeting.

That helped, but still something was objecting from my child within. *What could it be?* I wondered. The face of the committee chairperson flashed in my mind.

That was it. She reminded me of my perfectionistic mother, and I had been irritated with her at a meeting or two, but unwilling to admit it. I called a support-group friend and talked a few minutes about the chairperson's style. We talked about how I could respond when she made demands on me. I felt a lot better because I was doing the right thing by going to the meeting and by going with a healthy attitude.

Does this sound complicated? Once we get used to tuning into our child within, it's not difficult. Kerry's thought processes took only a few minutes. That's a small price to pay for getting in touch with our deeper needs and being able to take care of them.

King Baby attitudes. The childish child within may be communicating unhealthy attitudes by imitating the King Baby parent. If our parents were harsh, our child within is harsh with us. If our parents abused us emotionally, physically, or sexually, our child within tends to do the same thing. Some ACDFs even hit themselves and yell, "No! No! No!"

It's important to know what our typical self-talk messages are and how they sabotage us. We call ourselves names—"You idiot!" We scold ourselves with, "You're just like your mother." If someone could record us saying these things to ourselves, we would be horrified at the harshness in our voices. In support groups, we hear other people lash out at themselves, and we realize that we do the same thing.

3. Talk About Past and Present Feelings.

Anyone who was locked in a closet for thirty years would probably be afraid to come out even if the door were unlocked. There's too much light out there. In the same way, our child within is afraid to face buried feelings.

Yet talking about feelings relieves the pain, pressure, and isolation. A burden shared is cut in half as we allow others to come alongside us and nurture us.

We need to select our audiences carefully. It is important to choose a "safe" person, such as a listening friend, a therapist, or a support group. This step is risky for some of us—we may cry for the first time in our adult lives.

Here are some fears that hold us back.

Fear of hurt. We have to be patient with that childlike child within, who's afraid of how that light will hurt. It takes some people as long as three years in support groups or therapy to let that child express fears. We may have to reassure ourselves over and over that we will survive.

It takes courage to endure the hurt of some memories. When we accept this challenge, we find that God can sustain us and love us as much as if he were physically holding us in his arms and loving us. He doesn't want that child to stay locked in the closet forever, and neither do we.

Fear of rejection. We assume too often that others will reject us if they know how broken we are. We believe that they have their lives in order and that it's only we who don't.

Many other people have the same feelings of incompleteness that we have, and some are relieved to find out that we also have feet of clay. The more transparent we are, the more open they are to trust us and share with us.

Others may reject us because they expect us to maintain a facade of perfection. When we accept our limitations and admit them, we may need to explain to these people that we have no intention of living up to their standards. Standing up to these people isn't easy, as Karen discovered:

> My mother criticizes the way I discipline my kids. For a long time, I bought into the "bad-mother myth" that she had developed about me, and I believed I was a terrible, screaming mother.
>
> I've since discovered that I'm not much different from other mothers. My "problem" is that I'm not the perfectly calm textbook mom she has wanted me to be. Now that I think about it, she wasn't either.
>
> After three years in recovery, I told my mother:
> I do get frustrated with my kids, but I also have good times with them. When I yell at them, I later apologize. I've never been physically abusive. I have the same problems other moms have. I may not the "perfect mother" you expect me to be, but I'm working at being the best mom I can be. I think your remarks are uncalled for, and I would like for you to keep them to yourself.
>
> The next time we talked, she made another snide comment about my parenting. I repeated my entire lecture. How many times will it take?

When people reject you, or when you simply feel rejected, talk about it in a support group or with a recovering friend. If you're angry or hurt, say so. Help yourself see that this person's assessment may not be accurate and that other (and perhaps healthier) people love you.

Fear of memories.   Those who seem to fear memories most are the ACDFs who suffered physical or sexual abuse. According to the National Association for Children of Alcoholics, many children of alcoholics are victims of incest, child neglect, and other forms of violence and exploitation.[1] That's why it's not uncommon for persons in ACDF support groups to talk about intense victimization.

Many abuse victims are unable to remember anything that happened during early childhood. When memories do surface, they may come in pieces or as full scenes. Some people remember only smells or sounds, and dreams or conversations bring more of the memory back. Even then, many people aren't sure that what they remember is true, even though they may recall vivid details while they're fully awake. We have to trust that God will help us remember only what our conscious minds can handle and that he'll allow us to remember it only when we can handle it.

Even those of us who weren't abused tend to shut out the traumas of childhood. A simple feeling may surface and overwhelm each of us, and we're not sure why. As an adult, Candace visited her parents, whom she had not seen in several years.

> My parents figured I would sleep in the same bedroom I had had as a teenager. As soon as I was alone in that room, all those old feelings of depression and hopelessness overwhelmed me. I remembered sitting on the floor of my bedroom as a teenager listening to my parents argue, thinking that I would never get away from them. I used to turn up the stereo so that I couldn't hear anything.
>
> The night that I slept there as an adult, I clung to my pillow. I was already worried about my job, and being in my old bedroom made me more insecure than ever. The next night I made an excuse to stay in another room.
>
> This experience helped me because I was in denial about my childhood. I kept telling my support group that it hadn't been all that bad. I see now why I feel so depressed and hopeless at times—I grew up that way.

4. Nurture the Scared Child Within.

Our child within may have felt cut off, almost nonexistent. In recovery, we nourish that child back to life in the following ways.

Accept appropriate affection. Small children perceive love through physical affection, but we may not have received much physical affection as children in our dysfunctional homes. Now, as adults, we may find great comfort in being hugged and held by adults who understand us. Support groups or a caring church can be these physical arms of God, letting us know that we are loved and valued.

Use childlike comforts. On occasion, some members of the New Hope Support Group brought teddy bears to meetings. Other members thought it was unusual at first. Curt finally talked to them about it:

> I didn't know what to say, so I asked, "What's his name?" They had given their teddy bears cute names, like Cuddles and Buffy. Some of these stuffed animals were twenty years old and had ragged red ribbons or only one eye.
>
> I was embarrassed for the people who brought them. *Can't you leave them in the car?* I thought.
>
> Finally, I saw that there was something special going on with these stuffed animals. As their owners returned to their childhood to work things out, they nurtured themselves along the way.
>
> Once I got over being embarrassed, I realized I was jealous because they had returned to their childhood method of comfort so easily. The child within me thought it was great.

Indulge in childlike play. As we recover, we delight in activities that we loved as children, such as climbing trees, playing with modeling clay, or drawing with colored pens. We enjoy them again—only this time we are free of the tension that accompanied our play as children.

Childlike play also helps us relax during the emotionally taxing process of recovery. It requires us to step on the brakes of our behavior patterns, grind them to a halt, and then move in reverse. This is hard work, and we need to reward ourselves with "down time" in childlike play.

Sing about God's love.   Many hymns, Scripture songs, and simple childhood songs reassure us that God loves us. Singing "Jesus Loves Me" tells the child within that we too are the "little ones" that belong to Jesus. It's okay to let Jesus be strong while we are weak. This song helps us understand that God affirms us, loves us, and holds us in our pain.

Many of us sang "Jesus Loves Me" as confused children, and it's soothing to sing it again as recovering adults and absorb the truth of it. At a recent recovery conference, eight hundred people joined hands and sang this song together. We were moved to tears because we felt for the first time that Jesus was holding and loving the child within us.

Picture God's love.   By personalizing some of the Psalms, we can figuratively crawl into God's lap and have him hold us and rock us to sleep:

> He reached down from on high and took hold of me;
>   he drew me out of deep waters.
> He brought me out into a spacious place;
>   he rescued me because he delighted in me.
> Psalm 18:16, 19

Here's another vehicle that Jan uses to picture God's love for herself:

> A child-development specialist advised me to buy a picture of Jesus holding a child on his lap and give it to my daughter so that she would understand that God loves her. Sometimes when I'm alone, I sit on her bed and look at the picture myself. In it, Jesus touches that child so gently and holds his hand behind her head. He rubs his bearded cheek next to her cheek, and she looks

peaceful. I think about how God loves me the same way, and it comforts me.

Cry freely.   Even though tears were often taboo in our dysfunctional childhood families, in recovery we find the freedom to cry. A good cry releases the pressure in our holding tanks and allows the hurt, anger, and fear to escape. It breaks up the intensity of our recovery work and may even relieve headaches and muscle tension.

Tears aren't a sign that we are "losing it." Some wise person said that tears are prayers; indeed, they're the most honest prayers many of us have ever prayed. They are also a sign that our feelings are coming alive again. Crying is a preliminary step to being able to laugh and to trust.

Keep a journal.   Another healthy release is writing all kinds of feelings in a confidential book. The Psalms often sound like journaling, and we may begin as David did, with venomous comments—"But God will shoot them with arrows; suddenly they will be struck down" (Ps. 64:7). After David let go of these vindictive feelings, he concluded, "Let all the upright in heart praise him!" (Ps. 64:10b). This is a typical progression in the Psalms of David. He poured out his negative feelings and eventually surrendered them to God and praised him.

Nurturing the child within cannot, however, dominate our worlds. For example, the child within may need to cry over a sad memory, but the adult is getting up to make a sales presentation. The adult needs to put that child on hold, give the presentation, and then at an appropriate moment, give that child all the necessary time. We must consider the needs of the child within and meet them as well as we can.

Sometimes it's necessary to meet the child halfway. You may have the urge to go swimming, but if you leave your job, you'll get fired. Your child within may be telling you to balance your life with some fun, so you must substitute another activity that's fun. Talk to a jovial co-worker, put your feet up and relax during a break, or set aside time to go swimming on the weekend. Enjoy those feelings of innocence, and find a way to accommodate them even as you fulfill your adult responsibilities.

5. Set Limits on the King Baby in You.

Part of recovery is learning not to indulge the King Baby part of our child within: "Do not use your freedom to indulge the sinful nature" (Gal. 5:13a). Instead, we become wise, nurturing parents to that King Baby part of us. King Baby's two greatest problems are these:

Pain management. We understand that King Baby wants to control people and circumstances to keep from being hurt again. We keep this part of our inner child from striking out at people who intimidate us by learning to be assertive. We may even have to avoid these people until we have learned those skills.

In recovery, we refuse to manage pain with compulsions. If we need help with a compulsion, Twelve-Step groups or other support groups are available.

We ventilate fear and anger in healthy ways, such as these:

- We talk to a friend, support group, or therapist.
- We run or roller-skate or play basketball.
- We use a punching bag or throw pillows.
- We play a musical instrument vigorously.
- We write a letter of confrontation, but don't send it.
- We go to a lonely place, and shout one of those imprecatory Psalms (see Psalm 64:7, which we quoted earlier).

A *"me first"* mentality. We each examine our motives: Am I being manipulative? Do I have to be right all the time? Do I have to have my way because I'm selfish? Can I go out of my way to help others?

That last sentence sounds codependent, but it doesn't have to be. We still help others, but we don't do it to the point at which we diminish our own self-care.

Selfishness is different from self-care. Selfishness is thinking only of ourselves at the expense of others; self-care is doing what is best for our own well-being (for example, getting enough sleep or avoiding tempting situations). At times, self-care may inconvenience others, so we have to find a balance, in which others don't suffer needlessly.

We have a difficult time finding balance. We may have been self-sacrificing in the past, so we now we feel like being selfish. In the past, we hid our anger, and now we want to ventilate it freely. This is a normal tendency, and we need to find healthy ways to practice self-care and to express anger without hurting others.

If other people are used to our old self-sacrificing ways, they might be angry when we pull back. We have to stand up for ourselves with phrases such as, "I know this isn't convenient for you, but it's what I need to do." Even then, they may not understand.

You may be wondering . . .

Q *Isn't it unhealthy for my children to see me cry?*
A Our tears may make our spouses, friends, or children feel uncomfortable because they feel as if our sorrow is their fault or that they have to help us. It's wise to explain that our crying has nothing to do with their behavior, but that it's a positive release of sad feelings. This is a healthy model for children.

CHAPTER 13

What Could Go Wrong?

It is misleading to say that the recovery journey is filled only with rest areas (support-group meetings) and poignant reunions (discovering the child within). There are also mechanical failures (inner turmoil) and inclement weather (outsiders who discourage us). We may have days in which we spin our wheels in vain.

Yet, ups and downs are normal in recovery. We may be patient with a dysfunctional parent one day and sharp the next. The overall movement in recovery is upward, even though we get overwhelmed and resort to old behaviors at times.

We may even settle into a plateau of complacency. We feel frustrated because we aren't growing fast enough. *Is recovery worth the struggle?* we wonder. We "tune out" at support-group meetings and push people away. This plateau often occurs when we shrink from taking a major step of recovery. For one person, that step might be grieving over his older brother's suicide that his family never talked about. For another, it might be standing up for herself in a victimizing relationship. When we risk taking these fearful steps, we experience breakthroughs in our recovery, and we put the plateau behind us.

Identify Potential Hazards

An Alcoholics Anonymous saying pinpoints typical pitfall moments with the acronym: HALT. We are likely to stumble when we are

Hungry

Angry

Lonely

Tired

In these moments of physical and emotional depletion, we lose our perspective, and we tell ourselves, *I can't do anything right.* We think about practicing our compulsions and even forgetting about ACDF recovery.

Ileana tells how this almost happened to her:

> I was already angry with a co-worker because she had implied to my boss that I wasn't pulling my share of the workload. Then my friend Letitia called to cancel our lunch date. She had a valid excuse—she had to go home and check on her sick daughter. Letitia said she was sorry, and I knew she had a valid reason to cancel, but I still felt abandoned. I couldn't shake the anger and loneliness.
>
> I decided I would skip the ACDF meeting that night. *Maybe I'll go out for ice cream during my lunch hour,* I thought. *I'll get one of those huge sundaes. Then I'll feel better.*
>
> Then I thought of the HALT expression. No wonder I wanted to "pig out." I was angry at my co-worker and lonely for a friend.
>
> *Let's sort this out,* I thought, *and see how I can get my needs met legitimately.* First, I talked with my boss and corrected what my co-worker had said. (My boss had suspected the truth already.) Then I called Letitia and said, "I know you need to check on your daughter, but can I ride along with you? I need to talk to somebody today." That was fine with Letitia, and we enjoyed our time together.

Ileana saw her problem in the proper perspective and solved each part of it. As a result, she didn't eat a sundae

for lunch, or for dinner, either. She went to the ACDF
meeting that night and shared her victory.

Certain "hot situations" may spell trouble, and so we
prepare ourselves. Cathy has become skilled at this:

> I have a problem with volunteering too much, so,
> for the time being, I've quit attending meetings for all
> the groups I belong to, except one. Although I still at-
> tend a hospital auxiliary meeting, I leave to get a drink
> of water when they ask for volunteers. It sounds selfish,
> but I have to protect myself. This is a lot easier than
> picking up the pieces later when I lose my temper with
> my children because I'm angry that I volunteered when
> I shouldn't have.

Setbacks aren't all bad. They force us to use what we've
learned in recovery about problem solving. They are
achievement tests, so to speak, to see what we've learned so
far.

Internal Setbacks

Stuck in anger.   Some anger fuels our recovery because
it forces us to break out of denial. We express it in safe
places such as support groups. But we can't stay angry.
Holding onto anger slows down our recovery because we
channel energy into our anger, and that energy should be
channeled into recovery. We aren't using the anger; it's using us.

Recovery means facing that anger and releasing it. We
become stuck in anger when we replay past events in our
minds or when we think angrily of our parents just because someone cuts us off on the highway. We may get
stuck in anger because we think we'll never climb out of
our dysfunctionality. We don't yet believe that God can
and will help us overcome our unhealthy feelings and patterns. We don't understand recovery well enough to know
that it can work.

Being stuck in anger may also mean that we're not free of our parents yet. We need to talk, cry, journal, exercise, sing, shout—whatever helps us work through our anger without harming others or ourselves.

The "blame game."   It's unhealthy and unfair to blame our problems on our parents, on the church, or on the neighbor down the street. Blaming makes us bitter people. Living a life filled with "If only she hadn't . . ." and "It's his fault" keeps us from taking personal responsibility for our recovery. It chains us to spiritual immaturity.

Blaming parents is unfair also because most of our parents are ACDFs themselves. If we knew about the problems they had faced as children, we might be surprised at how relatively healthy they are.

Besides, the cliché is true: "They did the best they could." At AA meetings, recovering alcoholics often talk about how they tried to be good parents and how badly they blew it. They love their children and wish they had treated their children better. Perhaps these are your parents' thoughts as well.

Impatient for success.   "Shouldn't I be through this by now?" we ask. We're tired of feeling sad.

Some of us have unrealistic standards of how fast we should progress. We need to tone down our goals for ourselves and give ourselves time to heal. We'll never "arrive," but we will get better, which is the heart of the AA expression "Progress, not perfection."

Unable to accept parents.   We feel guilty when we don't forgive and accept those who have wronged us. Forgiveness is the "Christian thing to do," and we aren't doing it. Yet to announce that we have forgiven someone—even if only to ourselves—before we have worked through our hurts can result in superficial forgiveness. We feel guiltier than ever when the anger comes back.

Our goal is to forgive, yet forgiveness is often a by-product of working through repressed feelings and anger. After we have done this, we know exactly what actions or attitudes we are forgiving, and forgiveness can come from our depths.

Forgiveness is a process, not a one-time event. We move through anger and on to acceptance, which may fluctuate, especially if the ones we're forgiving still behave in dysfunctional ways. Here are Glenn's experiences:

> At Thanksgiving, my relatives put at least eight bottles of wine on the table, even though my mother is a recovering alcoholic and my sisters are alcoholics. Instead of wondering when they'll learn, I finally accepted this. My relatives aren't interested in recovery, and I'm not going to change them.
>
> Sometimes I don't do so well. Our family has a pattern of using subtle guilt and shame to get us to conform to family wishes. I can't stand it after a while, and I make an excuse to leave.
>
> Other times it's worse. When I talk on the phone to my mother, I snap at her even though she isn't saying anything particularly irritating. I tell her, "I've gotta go."
>
> "But we've only talked for three minutes," she'll say.
>
> I'm not mad at her exactly. Sometimes just hearing my mom's voice brings up a backlog of delayed grief, and I get tense. I don't want to be unkind, so I would rather quit talking to her than get angry.

Acceptance means that we quit trying to change our parents. Even if they're addicted and in denial of their addiction, we do little good to try to convince them to get recovery. Our former codependent ways and "fix-it" attitudes don't work. (Nevertheless, a formal intervention done by an entire family with the help of a professional can be a worthwhile effort.)

When we accept our parents, we open up the possibility of having a new relationship with them. We don't expect them to be Superdad or Supermom, but they are Gordon or Mary, people who have struggled. They are also people with whom we have much in common, people that we love.

External Setbacks

Family get-togethers. ACDF meetings at holiday times abound with discussions of how to act around relatives now that we're in recovery. Our new patterns of relating to people can confuse and even alienate relatives. It's as if we're singing a new song and they don't like its upbeat style. They may criticize our new singing style or badger us into singing in our former (dysfunctional) style.

Consider each invitation carefully. You may even want to remain noncommittal until you have had time to think it through. Ask yourself these questions:

- Do I want to do this?
- Is this mandatory?
- Is this good for me?
- Am I equipped to deal with the people and situations I'll face?
- Am I being worked into this by guilt?

When we're new in recovery or dealing with a particularly dominant relative, we may even have to take a year off from family outings. Maggie skipped the family Thanksgiving dinner because she knew that her uncle would be there. He had abused her as a child, and she was too angry at him to see him without creating a scene.

Richard had never worked up the courage to tell his parents that he didn't like pulling his children away from their presents on Christmas morning and driving to Grandma's. In recovery, he and his family saw Grandma at another time and stayed home on Christmas Day.

Sometimes it helps to talk to a friend, as Marsha did:

> My father called to say that he wanted to visit—he had even made his reservations already. He planned to stay two weeks! What could I do?
>
> I told him I would have to check my schedule. I hung up and called a support-group friend, Gail.
>
> Gail quizzed me gently. "Do you want to see him? Can you handle it?"
>
> "Yes, but not for two weeks."
>
> "How long do you want to see him?" Gail asked.
>
> "Two days is about what I can handle."
>
> "Suggest he stay two days. Tell him that is what's convenient for you."
>
> That's what I did, and the visit went well. I love my father, but I don't yet know how to respond to him. Normally he pushes my buttons, but this shorter visit was a good experience.

"Fixers." Beware of well-intentioned but uninformed advice givers who tell us their version of what God wants us to do. Those who know nothing about recovery push us to forget the past, take control of our lives, and move on. They don't understand the importance of ventilating emotions.

Telling parents about our recovery. As we recover, we may want to tell our parents about our recovery work. Here are some examples of key elements to include in such a session:

- "I'm having certain problems in life." (Be specific, using the wording of the ACDF characteristics if you like. Talk about illnesses or a depression that got your attention.)
- "I'm going to a support group" (or to therapy).
- "I'm discovering new aspects of myself" (your child within) "and new ways of coping with problems."

- "I'm releasing the hurts I've felt from the past."
- "My life is better because of my recovery."

We first tell our parents about the problems that got our attention so that they understand why recovery is important. They would want us to correct something that would keep us from having a successful marriage, career, or parenting experience. This can help them see that we're not searching for people to condemn, just for answers to our problems.

Yet no matter how carefully this is worded, parents usually feel that they're being blamed. They may feel defensive, and deny the family's dysfunctionality. Don't be surprised if they pressure you or try to convince you that you're wrong. When they find that they are unable to convince you, they may even ridicule you or have nothing to do with you.

Angela, an ACDF, introduced the subject to her parents by saying that she was going to therapy. Her mother stopped her by saying, "I certainly hope your father and I haven't contributed to this problem." Angela could see that she was not going to be heard, so she dropped the subject.

Even if your parents are recovering alcoholics, they may not want to hear about your recovery. They feel ashamed of their past and the family's dysfunctionality, even if you congratulate them on their sobriety. No matter how your parents respond, you will no doubt perspire and shake as you have done only a few other times in your life.

Fruitfulness is the key. If talking with parents will further your recovery, consider it. Carla, a recovering ACDF, didn't want to talk to her parents about the family's dysfunctionality, but she did want them to understand why she behaved so differently. She told them a little at a time. When they asked her repeatedly to help them out but didn't ask the other children, she explained, "I'm not the family hero, Mom. There are other kids in this family, and they can help too." When her mother tried to get her to talk to her brother about reuniting with his wife, Carla said, "I'm not getting triangulated with you and Ben anymore. If you want to tell him something, call him."

Confronting parents. This isn't mandatory, and most ACDFs don't do it. Motives can be difficult to sort out. Sometimes we want to confront parents out of subtle feelings of revenge: "They hurt me; now I'll hurt them." Seeking revenge shows that we are stuck in anger and not focusing on our own recovery.

Some ACDFs, however, feel that confronting parents with the details of the family's dysfunctionality is necessary for their own recovery. This seems to be particularly true with families in which the dysfunctionality was more discreet than usual. Perhaps the family was respected and admired publicly, or one child was abused by a parent but no one admitted it. In these circumstances, ACDFs have trouble believing the dysfunctionality themselves, and they need parents or siblings to admit that their "wonderful" families were not all that they pretended to be.

A confrontation often turns out the way it did for Tom, the Christian therapist whose father was a minister.

> I brought up little bits, but they kept saying I had a good childhood and that they wanted to live out their years in peace. I feel angry about that. I need to work through my past. I need to talk to them about this. It's as if the air won't be clear until I do.
>
> I can't be myself around them anymore. I disagreed with Dad at a birthday party not too long ago, and we had a shouting match. Then everything got quiet.
>
> Finally, someone said, "Let's open the presents."
>
> Later that day, my older brother scolded me and said I should be more thankful for my parents. One sister won't talk about it, and the other says she's ashamed of me for bringing it up.

Before I left, my dad and my brother told me not to make waves with the family. I explained that I'm not trying to stir up dissension, but that I'm dealing with past problems that affect me today. When I told my dad how I was overcoming my sexual addiction and my workaholism, he said he respected me for that. That ounce of encouragement helped so much.

If parents are in denial, as Tom's are, it might be as fruitful to talk to someone besides parents such as brothers or sisters in recovery or understanding aunts, uncles, or grandparents. In confrontation, the most important thing is to speak out the truth and have it validated.

Many ACDFs confront their parents indirectly. They write their confrontations in their journals, or even in letters, which they never send. Others confront their parents by telling their support groups what they would like to say. Even though the parents aren't present, anger is released, and the truth is revealed.

You may be wondering . . .

Q *Do I still need to deal with these issues if my parents are deceased? If so, what difference does it make?*

A The death of one or both parents doesn't diminish the effect that a dysfunctional upbringing has on you as an adult, but it does create a few extra challenges in recovery. Our culture tends to deify dead persons, so you may feel guilty for being angry with them. Siblings particularly may resent you for working through recovery, because they have glorified your parents and have reprogrammed their own memories. Give yourself permission to work through the anger and hurt. As you recover, you'll be more equipped to be at peace with the memory of your parents.

Q *Why do so many people get divorced when they start recovery work?*

A Many ACDFs do get divorced and have increased problems with their families, their jobs, or their relationships while working through recovery. The pain of the past becomes real, and they "bleed" onto innocent people by blaming and projecting anger onto them.

Yet recovery doesn't create these problems. They are rooted in dysfunctionality, which makes it difficult to communicate with others. Recovery can accent the problems because it teaches us what is sick about our behavior and about the ways people treat each other. We become less tolerant of our poor communication and of our dysfunctional family characteristics. Marriages usually stay together when recovering ACDFs do the following:

- concentrate on their recovery
- admit problems without blaming their spouses
- recognize that they can't control their spouses' behavior
- realize that their spouses may not understand recovery
- give the spouse capsuled reports of their improvement and goals
- obtain marriage counseling when necessary

Section 4

The Partners
in Our Recovery

CHAPTER 14

Feeling Safe at Church

Before recovery, our typical answer to people at church who asked us how we were, was, "I'm fine." Some of us even chirped phrases such as, "Praise the Lord! Life is wonderful!"

At a recovery conference, one ACDF suggested that when she answered, "Fine," she actually meant this:

F = fouled up

I = insecure

N = neurotic

E = emotionally unbalanced

We're good at saying we're "fine" when we're dying spiritually, emotionally, and physically. We know there is pain in our hearts, but we think that Christians always have "their little ducks in a row."

Donna, the church secretary in the first chapter, confesses that she had a double life: her "daytime identity" and her "nighttime identity."

> At work, I never let people know I was upset. If I had to stay late, I acted cheerful about it. At home, I released my pent-up anger because I knew my husband would stick with me no matter what I said. I yelled at him and my son, and even threw things at them. The people at church were shocked when I told them about my explosive behavior at home. I see now that my nighttime identity was my outlet. I had to "let down my hair" somewhere because my inner needs weren't being met. I was trying to please too many people.

ACDFs Populate the Church

As ACDFs, we are the "hidden wounded" in the church, as we hide our hurts behind our careful facades. We are so blind to these wounds that we pity the "obviously wounded"—those with illnesses, physical limitations, and financial problems. We think, *I'm sure glad that's not me. I'm glad I'm together.*

At other times we envy these "obviously wounded": *Look at how the church prays for them and gives them cash love-gifts.* No one offers *us* help because they don't know we are hurting.

We wear our Teflon℠ masks at church so that when some comment gouges us, it leaves no marks. We steel ourselves for so long that even the sharpest treatment seems to leave us untouched.

As long as we don't admit that we're hurting, we don't allow God to touch the unresolved areas of our life. Yet it's so difficult to admit the extent of our hurt and our dysfunctionality to others, especially to church people—and even more so if they look up to us.

Both of us (Curt and Jan) had wanted for a year to attend church-related support groups but did not do so out of fear. What would Christians think of a Christian therapist who had panic attacks? about a pastor's wife who was mad at God? Once we became desperate, we finally did attend those groups, but we didn't reveal our "lofty" positions for several months, until we felt safe.

The perfect masks that we all wear make it difficult for people to believe that the church could be populated by so many ACDFs. Are there really so many "losers," as we've been called, among the members, and even among the leaders, in their church?

A Christian organization called Focus on the Family broadcast its first radio program about adult children of alcoholics in November 1988, because it had received so many requests for programs on that topic. In fact, it had received more requests from its listeners for this topic than for all other topics combined. Even among this family-oriented audience with traditional values, problems of dysfunctionality were surfacing.

The rate at which Christian ACDF support groups are growing is further proof. Curt began compiling a list of these groups from the response to that broadcast, and as of 1991, there were more than two thousand support groups. One woman in Canada called to find out how to start a group because she was traveling two and one-half hours each way to attend a secular ACA group. There are many others like her.

Fitting In at Church

Even though recovery helps our spiritual lives, it doesn't always help our church lives. As we recover, we learn to talk about God and about our problems more openly and honestly, which makes others at church feel uncomfortable. Then *we* feel awkward too. We're wiping clean those smoked-glass images of God, and we want to tell our church friends. We're excited, but will they understand? Unfortunately, Roger's experience isn't an uncommon one:

> I had always been a staunch church member, but I resigned from church leadership to focus on my ACDF recovery. I got used to support groups, in which we accepted each other even though we confessed our ugliest thoughts and darkest sins. I liked connecting with people on a deeper level. I tried to correct my warped view of Scripture, and God became so much more real to me as a parent.
>
> As my recovery progressed, I felt more and more uneasy about church programs and worship services. Before my recovery, I had gotten so much out of them,

but now they seemed like child's play. I longed to hear the pastor preach about "real" problems, like our doubts and fears about God. I longed to have a stirring conversation with someone in the hall after church.

I found that I wasn't fitting in as well. I no longer considered issues so "black and white," perhaps because my recovery showed me that I didn't know the answers. I also no longer accepted everything the pastor said. I asked questions, which made a few people uncomfortable.

I'm never sure how much I should talk about my recovery. Would it shock church members that their former board chairman was no longer a "looking-good Christian"?

It's important that ACDFs and the church don't lose confidence in each other. We need each other. The church can help us with recovery by channeling us into service, by helping us understand the Bible, by providing a setting for corporate worship.

Our contribution is that we bring a sense of reality to the church. As nursery workers, choir members, and Bible teachers, we connect with those who are hurting, and we bring a deeper sense of caring. In recovery, we become willing to take off our masks—even at church—and we free others to do the same.

Here are some attitudes that may help you feel that you fit in at church.

Abandon your "church identity." We wear a "church identity" when we hide our anger in order to be acceptable. We edit less-than-Christian comments out of our speech so that we mistakenly conclude that we have erased them from our thoughts as well. At an inopportune moment, these angry thoughts appear in boldface print at the top of the page for the whole world to see.

We may also edit out neutral thoughts when we're wearing our "church identities." We don't say what we think, because we want to please others. Test yourself for a few days, and listen to the thoughts that you don't dare verbalize to others because you think, *I can't say that. It sounds so unchristian.* This editing promotes the "Jekyll and Hyde" identity that Donna, the church secretary, used.

In recovery, we listen to angry thoughts and figure out calm, nonthreatening ways to ventilate them. We try as much as possible not to say one thing when we feel the opposite. When someone asks, "How are you?" we don't lie and say we're fine if we're not. We offer the truth in subtle form:

"I'm growing. Sometimes it's not fun."

"God's strength today is sufficient."

"I'm hanging in there."

The reward for being honest, yet calm, is that we find the serenity we've been looking for.

It can be interesting to challenge others to abandon their church identities. When we ask other church members, "How are you?" we gently demand candid answers. If they say they're fine, we say, "No, tell me—how are you really doing?" Some may spill their frustration and even their anger with life. Others may begin to cry. Still others make a mental note that we reached below the surface, and in the future they either seek us out or stay away from us.

Recognize that no child of God is more "worthy" than another. Many of us serve at church out of codependent motives, struggling to be good enough. We may even secretly feel that God loves those who serve unselfishly more than he loves us.

Every person has worth in God's eyes. Here's how Dawn came to understand this:

In the "old days," before recovery, I volunteered for everything. I led children's church even though I wasn't by nature an organizer. I sang in the choir, I baked lots of zucchini bread for continental breakfasts.

Recovery forced me to shed my "looking-good kid" image and to be honest. Now I see that I was trying to earn God's love. I felt inferior to the other people at church, who gave more money than I did, who organized events so well. I felt that God loved them more than he loved me. I realized that my parents had treated us kids that way. Whoever did the most was loved the most. For years, I was the "adjuster child," and I never stood out like my sister, the "responsible child." As an adult, I tried to fill her role. I thought I had finally grown up.

Now I see how silly that is. I believe that God loves me for *me* and that he's bringing me along as fast as I can follow. I'm now interested in a ministry to the homeless, and I've found a friend who's a true organizer to help me. The choir and the education committee are disappointed that I won't be serving with them, but it's important that I serve God from my heart. For once, I'm following the path that I sense God wants me to take, rather than listening to everyone else.

Develop thick skin.   Since our recovery teaches us not to take ourselves so seriously, we are no longer as offended by other people's remarks or put-downs. Remember the HALT acronym? Those offensive people could be hungry, angry, lonely, or tired. Most people are so caught up in their own problems that they don't have the energy to pick on us intentionally.

Besides, those in our families, neighborhoods, jobs, and churches also act out of their own dysfunctional family issues. When they try to control us or when they reject us, it may have nothing to do with what we've done. Often, it has everything to do with an insignificant detail, such as a physical feature we have that reminds them of one of their parents.

This doesn't mean that we bury hurtful church situations. We talk about them in a support group or bounce them off a friend. There, we can figure out whether we should confront these situations or disregard them. Are these people's words or actions injuring us, or just irritating us? Is confrontation appropriate or helpful?

Make worship an important part of your life.   Relish the songs and hymns that emphasize God's greatness, his love, his forgiveness. As we sing about his ability to help us and our desire to grow in him, we connect with God in a deeper way. Worship is a powerful vehicle to negate the nagging doubts or tones of religious shame many of us have experienced.

Worship is a time to seek God and acknowledge that he loves us. We practice the presence of God: "And surely I am with you always, to the very end of the age" (Matt. 28:20b). Worship moves us beyond the cognitive level of understanding and helps us believe in our hearts that God is our very capable and powerful parent.

For some, meaningful worship means singing more songs in the shower. Others will want to play recordings of praise music in the car. Still others will set up their own private times of worship, which will make them more attentive in the worship services at church.

You may be wondering . . .

Q   *What if I don't feel like going to church anymore?*
A   Some ACDFs feel that way. Because of the high quality of time we spend in support groups, we enjoy intimacy and honest talk about real-life issues. When we don't find the same quality at church, we feel frustrated. We may even shun large services with lecturers and

little interaction. This is not an abnormal feeling in recovery.

We don't want to isolate ourselves from the church — especially when we're learning in recovery not to solve our problems by isolating ourselves!

Talk to your pastor about your recovery experiences. Ask your pastor to address anger, forgiveness, even your "crisis of faith" issues in sermons. As you've discovered in support groups, people learn more from discussion than from lecture, but lecture transmits large amounts of information in a short time. So try to discuss the sermons with others so that you can absorb the information well.

You may need to attend another church. Make certain you know what you're looking for, such as fellowship with people your age or a worship style that helps your recovery. No church will have everything you're looking for, and it can be lonely to "church shop."

CHAPTER 15

Support Groups:
Bearing Each Other's Burdens

"The church should be a hospital for sinners, not a museum for saints," said some perceptive Christian years ago. If churches are hospitals, then support groups are the intensive care unit. In support groups, you'll find medication (books and tapes), adequate facilities (circles of chairs, not rows), and highly equipped personnel (other ACDFs).

A support group provides a setting in which we can talk through our problems openly and honestly in the safe environment of others like ourselves. The sharing of feelings and experiences are welcome, no matter how ugly.

To clarify this purpose, we need to understand what a support group is not:

- a Bible study, though Scripture may be used
- group therapy, though there may be interaction
- a gripe session, though hurts are shared
- a screaming session, though anger is often expressed
- a rehashing of the past, though past events may be related
- an emotional scene, though some members may cry and hug

In short, support groups provide what we've never had: a safe place to talk, to trust, to feel.

Nonexperts Excel in an Era of Experts

Throughout history, people have gathered to listen, to talk, and to solve their problems together. Mothers shared insights as they washed their clothes in the river; hunters swapped stories over campfires.

As knowledge has become more specialized, however, we have assumed that only experts in certain fields can help us. Before Alcoholics Anonymous was created in 1935, experts proposed various solutions for alcoholism, but nothing worked:

- The medical community medicated alcoholism with drugs to stop the physical act of drinking. They hoped that would cure the habit, but it didn't.
- The psychological community helped alcoholics resolve problem issues so that they would no longer need to drink and would thus be "cured." This didn't work because alcoholics had formed lifelong habits of using alcohol to manage pain.
- The religious community urged alcoholics to call on God to miraculously stop the craving for alcohol. Like the other solutions, this worked for a few, but not for the many.[1]

This lack of success left people like Bill Wilson, a New York stockbroker, and Dr. Bob Smith, an Akron physician, feeling hopeless. Finally, Bill stopped his drinking through a spiritual experience he had after meeting with a friend who was a medical doctor. Yet when Bill went to Akron on business, he felt the need to drink, so he used the method he had used in New York—talking with another alcoholic. That alcoholic was Dr. Bob, who then also became sober, and they began visiting alcoholics at a local hospital. These recovering alcoholics met together, later calling themselves Alcoholics Anonymous.[2]

Bill Wilson and the early groups developed the Twelve Steps as a spiritual path to recovery (see Appendix 2). One of the reasons the Twelve-Step progression worked was that it combined all three of the previous approaches:

Physical: The alcoholic became accountable to the group to avoid drinking just one day at a time.

Psychological: The alcoholic dealt with personal defects of character and underlying issues. AA, as a support group, reinforced those who stayed sober and accepted practicing alcoholics as long as they wished to get better.

Spiritual: The alcoholic surrendered to a Higher Power and worked on personal defects of character.

These pioneering "nonexperts" used various tools, such as anonymity and confidentiality, to insure the safety necessary for alcoholics to get better (see "The Twelve Traditions" in Appendix 2). Over the years, the AA model has become the most successful method for treating alcoholism, and says *Newsweek,* "There are . . . few, if any, alcohol treatment centers in the United States that do not funnel their outpatients into AA."[3]

Those with other compulsions have found that the AA methods work for them as well. Now there are many Twelve-Step groups, including Cocaine Anonymous, Debtors Anonymous, Emotional Health Anonymous, Families Anonymous, Gamblers Anonymous, Narcotics Anonymous, Overeaters Anonymous, Parents Anonymous (for abusive parents), Smokers Anonymous, and Sexaholics Anonymous. The original Adult Children of Alcoholics groups also followed this pattern. All these groups adapted the Twelve Steps slightly for their particular compulsion, and all groups have used the Twelve Traditions.

What makes this method so powerful? The Twelve-Step groups have provided places of safety through their acceptance and rigorous honesty.

Safety

Church-related support groups work as the intensive care units of the church-hospital because they are safe. Confidentiality and anonymity ensure us that we can reveal our worst secrets without having them repeated. We hear others share similar secrets, and we no longer feel alone in the dysfunctional ways we act.

Support-group members gather as nonprofessionals with no designs to "fix" each other. The "no cross talk" rule (no interrupting while someone else is sharing) means that we listen to others who have the same problems without offering opinions and mini-sermons. No one makes us feel intimidated or inadequate, saying, "You're a Christian. You shouldn't feel that way!"

It's odd how much we are helped by listening to others. Hearing their stories challenges our mental ruts. We recognize that we struggle with the same things that other people struggle with. Here is one of Howard's experiences:

> At one meeting, a guy shared that he often got out of healthy romantic relationships for no reason. When some little thing went wrong, he jumped ship. I thought, *That's silly. I can't relate to that.*
>
> The next day, I looked at my dating history. I realized I had done the same thing several times. It was so obvious that I wondered how I could have missed it. I had missed it because it had seemed so unchristian. *Aren't Christians supposed to be committed people who stick things out?* I couldn't admit that I wasn't able to stay committed in a relationship. This was the first of many subconscious feelings I found that I had suppressed because they weren't "Christian."

The safety of support groups lets us try out feelings we buried long ago. As an "adjuster" (see Chapter 5), Anita never got angry, even though she lived with a controlling husband and two rebellious teenage sons. In the safety of a support group, Anita tasted anger for the first time:

> As people talked, they seemed to mention how mean their fathers were. I kept thinking, *What are their problems? Why didn't they tune it out?*
>
> Then someone repeated the exact phrase my dad used to say, and I heaved a loud sigh. This was unusual, because I'm the quiet one. Everyone looked at me in surprise.
>
> The leader said, "Anita, do you want to be next?"
>
> I sat silent for a few minutes. I felt as if pine cones were growing in my throat, and I couldn't have talked even if I had wanted to. The tears began to flow.
>
> Then I balled my hand into a fist and gently pounded my knee. "Why did my father talk to me that way?" I rasped. "I was such a good girl. I never talked back to him like my sister did." I couldn't quit crying, and no one said anything for several minutes.
>
> I had never acted that way in the group before. After the meeting, everybody talked to me and comforted me. At moments, I loved their comfort and ate it up. At other moments, I wanted to say, "Please leave me alone." I forced myself to sit through their encouragement. It was scary to be angry. It was scary to be encouraged.

Anita's behavior may not seem angry compared to our own expressions of anger, but to sweet, smiling adjuster Anita, it was rage. Later that night, she again recalled how her father had treated her, and her legs broke out in welts. Anger, even this mild form, was so foreign to her that her body reacted to it. She was at last shattering the dysfunctional family rules: *don't talk back, don't let others encourage you,* and *don't get angry*—all of which are corollaries of *don't talk, don't trust, don't feel.*

Support-Group–Style Honesty

A lot of before-and-after-church talk is the news-weather-and-sports variety: "Did you see that big game yesterday?" "I like your new dress." We all find it difficult to talk about our faith and our feelings.

That's why some people find support-group–style honesty refreshing. Yet it can be shocking and even offensive at first to hear others share confused and angry feelings. In time, we understand that this can be the first step to healing.

Curt's first visit to a support group surprised him:

> Everything was going well when the guy next to me (I'll call him Darrell) said, "I'm mad at God."
>
> I was shocked! No one else took it too hard, though, and, being a placater, I smiled at Darrell. *At least he's honest,* I thought.
>
> I was also intrigued by the situation. There we sat on church-owned chairs in a church classroom, and this guy said he was mad at God. Secretly, I had sometimes felt that kind of anger at God, too, but I had never admitted it to anyone—especially in a church building! *Boy, does this guy have guts,* I thought.
>
> Near the end of his sharing time, Darrell broke down in tears. He explained that he felt that God—in the form of his parents—never reached out to him.
>
> "My parents were so cold," he said. "They never told me they loved me. I felt alone and abandoned. They gave me money and everything I needed, but they never hugged me or touched me. I wasn't a bad kid. It wasn't fair that they ignored me."
>
> It dawned on me that something powerful was happening. These were honest people who were stating honest feelings and were finding acceptance from other Christians.
>
> When my turn came, I mumbled that perhaps I had felt mad at God, too. "Sometimes I don't understand the way he works," I told the group.

I rambled for a few minutes until I recalled the Scripture that says that nobody understands the mind of God: "Who has understood the mind of the Lord, or instructed him as his counselor?" (Isa. 40:13). As I talked, something happened. I felt some sense of relief. I was a little less angry, and I began thinking that I could accept the fact that I didn't understand God. This was the start of a more genuine relationship with him.

Darrell could have easily denied his anger toward God and wandered from his faith. Instead, he found a place to talk about it. He knew he wanted to be close to God, and this admission was the first step in understanding that God loved him. Because Curt got to view this process, he was able to deal with the same problem in the same healthy way.

Once you experience such honesty, you may become hooked on it—not because of its drama, but because of its healing. Your heart feels refreshed because you see God working in your life. You realize that he can even replace those crazy feelings with trust in him and a deep, abiding love for him.

Why Honesty Is So Important

Can you imagine what would happen in most Bible studies if someone like Darrell shared that he was mad at God? Many of those attending would get upset. Darrell knew that, of course, so he kept quiet. He sat in church many Sundays, thinking that he would explode if he didn't blurt out his true feelings. Some of us, as well, sit in church ready to explode because we can't pray anymore and we feel like worthless Christians. (We're not advocating a disrespect for God, but it's important to face ugly feelings so that our relationships with God can be healed.)

We don't dare express these feelings to our Christian friends. We are afraid they would respond to such outbursts with, "I'll pray for you," or, "Let's talk to the pastor," or even, "The devil is after you. We need to claim the victory here."

These friends wouldn't be wrong to emphasize prayer, direction, and self-control, but we need something more. We need for these friends to hear our hurt and respond to it. Without it, we are like patients with deep stab wounds being dressed by a stone-faced nurse. We need more than bandaging; we need tenderness and recognition of our hurt.

God has used support groups as a vehicle for his tenderness, as evidenced by the hugging that goes on after meetings. Even during the sharing, hands are squeezed, backs are patted, and tissues are passed. (Verbal interruptions are not allowed during the sharing time.)

The other ingredient that we sorely need is recognition of our honesty. We've hidden our true feelings for such a long time that it takes courage to step out of denial and come clean. We are more likely to risk being so honest when we are rewarded for it, which support groups do well with tears, empathetic looks, and even appropriate laughter. We leave meetings feeling understood and appreciated.

This honesty helps us form remarkably close bonds that knock down the walls that we have built around ourselves. Few people, even God, have ever penetrated our walls. As we talk about deeper issues, we connect with people for the first time. After we find that connecting with people is so exhilarating, we risk connecting with God as well.

How to Kill a Support Group: "Fixing"

Because Christianity is "the way, the truth, and the life," and Christians know the value of helping others, it's easy for us to "fix" each other. We have listened to so many sermons and tapes, and have read so many books, that we're sure we have the solutions to other people's problems. For many of us, our "helpful spirit" has turned into feelings of grandiosity—we have an answer for everything. Jan found this to be true.

I had been a pastor's wife for twelve years when I began attending a support group. In those years, I had done a lot of armchair counseling, and people had always thanked me for helping them so much. I figured I was pretty good at it.

I loved how the support group helped me understand myself, but I hated how it didn't allow me to "help" others. I found myself constantly thinking that if that person would just read a certain self-help book, he or she would be okay. *Was that "fixing"*? I wondered.

The "no cross talk" rule drove me crazy. Every time someone talked about a problem, I wanted to interrupt and tell that person about a Bible verse that would solve it. I finally placed my hand over my mouth to remind myself to keep quiet and listen.

I learned some astounding things from this. First, I learned what a know-it-all responsible child/placater I am. I honestly thought I could solve the problems of the people in my group. Then it hit me: If reading those books was such a great idea, why hadn't it worked for me? If I had so many "answers," why was I so broken? I realized that I had never worked through my problems. In the support group, I got to watch others work through problems week after week, until I began doing it myself.

As I focused on what others in my support group were saying, instead of on planning what I wanted to say in my sharing time, I was touched by their lives. Major breakthroughs in my attitudes occurred because other people's lives became a mirror to show me how dysfunctionally I was acting. Some of those people were also tall, sturdy signposts that showed me how to change my behavior. Never have so many people influenced me to change my life with so little intention of doing so.

Jan would have missed all this if she hadn't obeyed the standard support-group rule of "no fixing." This is the most difficult problem that longtime Christians have in support groups. Here are some helpful tips for those of us who are hard-core "fixers":

- We remember that our job as support-group members is to share about ourselves and our ACDF issues.
- We don't "play doctor" by using our own sharing times to offer ideas to others, even in subtle ways.
- We quiet the King Baby in us that is sure we have the answers, and we consider that someone else's seemingly silly solution just might work.
- We affirm others with actions, not with words. We hug them or pray with them, but we don't offer either of these in a "quick fix" way. It's tempting to pat them on the hand and say, "You're okay now, aren't you?" No, they're not okay. It will take a while to work through the problem.
- If others ask us for advice after the meeting, we tell them what worked for us, but we don't guarantee it will work for anyone else.

Believing that others can find their own solutions builds their confidence. As we respect another person's capacity to respond to the Holy Spirit, we build the church's sense of community as a "priesthood" of all believers (2 Pet. 2:9).

Support groups also provide an important puzzle piece in the church's educational program. In Bible studies and worship services, we're taught God's Word and how it applies to our lives, but in support groups, these truths sink in as we compare them to our experiences. The truths of

God's Word finally connect with our wounded spirits. In those other settings, we're told how we should change, but in support groups, we're loved and accepted for who we already are in Christ.

You may be wondering . . .

Q   *Is AA a Christian organization?*

A   Alcoholics Anonymous is not a distinctly Christian organization. The phrase "Higher Power" originally referred to God,[4] but the use of inclusive language began to draw agnostics[5] as well. Eventually, Jews, Hindus, Muslims, and Buddhists joined the fellowship,[6] which made the writers of *Alcoholics Anonymous* (also called the Big Book) glad because they wanted alcoholics of all faiths to recover.

The Big Book is sprinkled with the words *God, faith,* and *spiritual,* but faith in Christ is not mentioned. AA is spiritual in that it reminds alcoholics to allow their spiritual natures to participate in alcohol recovery, but its purpose is to help them find sobriety, not a specific faith.

Various Christian traditions have reacted differently to AA. When the Big Book was published, clergyman Dr. Harry Emerson Fosdick reviewed it with approval.[7] Today some churches endorse Twelve-Step groups so wholeheartedly that they go out of their way to have Twelve-Step meetings held at their facilities. However, some Christians have dismissed Twelve-Step meetings as "New Age" and maintain that the Higher Power is Satan. In recent years, atheists have objected to AA, saying that sobriety is a separate issue from spirituality. They have formed their own network, Secular Organizations for Sobriety (SOS).

Q *Can I talk about my faith at secular Twelve-Step meetings?*
A While most Twelve-Step meetings are secular, meaning that they have no religious overtones, it's not unusual for some people at meetings to name their
   Higher Power as Jesus. It's also not unusual for others
   to mention in their sharing times that they don't like it
   when Christians "act like AA is church." (Technically,
   this is cross talk, but it's defended as merely the sharing
   of feelings.) Different meetings vary greatly in tone.

   Christians can and do find support from secular
   Twelve-Step meetings. We recommend that you find
   one that meets your needs, particularly if there are no
   Christian meetings in your area. Those beginning addiction recovery usually find it mandatory to do as AA
   recommends: attend at least one meeting a day for
   thirty days.

Q *Why do some Twelve-Step people talk about the Twelve-Steps
   as if they were the Ten Commandments and the Big Book as
   if it were the Bible?*
A This near-reverence for AA tools comes from the dra-
   matic improvement that recovery has made on their
   lives. It's as if they were once held captive in the teeth
   of a dragon who was writhing his head at tremendous
   speeds, and now they're free. They've perhaps never
   read the Bible, but they did read biblical principles in
   the Big Book. It's their first taste of faith, and absorb-
   ing it has released them from the dragon.

CHAPTER 16

How To Start a Church-Related ACDF Support Group

The excitement was high as the New Hope Support Group formed at the First Evangelical Free Church in Fullerton, California. These first attendees had been part of Liontamers, the church's addiction recovery group. They had also attended secular ACA groups, but they wanted to integrate their recovery with their faith. They wanted to talk about God openly and get rid of their distortions. They wanted to learn how to stop being "looking-good Christians."

New Hope started with 10 people, but within two months, 25 people were attending. Within two years, 60 were attending. At this writing, New Hope has about 250 members, with one-third coming from nonalcoholic backgrounds.

This same rate of growth is so widespread that we hope that most churches in America will develop ACDF support groups in the next twenty years. This can easily happen if groups continue to multiply at the current rate.

Perhaps you believe that God wants you to start a support group in your church or community. Here are some steps to consider.

1. Attend a Church-Related ACDF Support Group.

The best way to understand support groups is to experience them. Participate regularly and work on your recovery. After you have attended for a while, ask to assist a small-group leader. Then ask to lead one on your own.

This internship approach helps avoid the most frequent problem with most groups: they start fast and die fast. The core group has had little recovery, so that when eighty people show up, the group feels overwhelmed and quickly becomes discouraged. Participating in a group helps you with your own recovery and prepares you for problems.

Leading other groups at church doesn't automatically qualify you as a support-group leader, because the tone and purpose are so different. Other groups often meet to seek solutions; support-group members often know the solutions but need a place to reflect on them so they can put them into action.

2. Talk to Your Pastor.

Groups that start without the backing of their pastors usually don't last. Even groups that start with the quasi-acceptance of their pastors are short-lived. Too often, groups get a go-ahead from pastors who don't understand ACDF issues or how support groups are different from other church groups.

Then, church members visit the group and get upset with the blatant honesty they find. They ask the pastor, "Do you realize what's going on in that group?" The pastor doesn't.

Or a deaconess will report to the church board: "Someone said a dirty word in that support group. I was offended, and I said so. They asked *me* not to interrupt!" (See the second question at the end of this chapter.) Then the pastor says that the group can't continue if this behavior occurs again.

To avoid this, tell the pastor in the beginning exactly what goes on. Don't candy-coat it. Show the pastor the materials you plan to use, and talk about how the meetings are conducted. (See Appendix 1 for an example.)

If the pastor isn't receptive, consider forming the group in a person's home. Many Christian ACDF groups now meet in homes—some of them with more than seventy attendees—because churches haven't given them approval to use church facilities. This occurs because many churches misunderstand ACDF recovery, especially the importance of processing anger and reparenting the inner child. Most of these churches aren't rejecting recovery; they're simply not informed of its part in spiritual growth.

If you don't know how to explain ACDF issues or support groups to your pastor, ask a more experienced group-leader in your area to help you. Give the pastor some literature that explains both ACDF issues and support groups. Pastors are busy people, so make it as easy as possible for them to understand what you're trying to do.

3. Set Your Format.

Many church-related recovery networks are springing up, in addition to secular Twelve-Step groups. These networks have come up with different format designs because they see recovery differently. Consider how each format might work with your potential group members and your resource people.

It's easy to get sidetracked from our recovery if we argue about which format is best. One reason that the Twelve-Step movement has insisted on one structure is that quibbling over format plays into our dysfunctionality. It distracts us from our recovery and may even kill the group. Use any format that stays close to the Twelve-Step guidelines for sharing, such as anonymity, confidentiality, and "no cross talk."

Here are some format issues to consider.

Group ground rules. Form some friendly-sounding guidelines for support-group discussion. Typical ground rules include accepting those who cry or get angry, not "fixing" others, focusing on one's own feelings, and not blaming others. (See Appendix 1).

Confidentiality is often explained with this saying: "What's said here stays here." A support group is no place for printed prayer lists or paper-thin walls. Groups bend over backward to create an atmosphere of safety.

As a group grows, it may need a guideline that limits sharing to three to five minutes so that everyone gets a chance to talk.

"No cross talk" means that no one interrupts another, even to ask a question. This especially helps quiet people gather their thoughts and ensures that people who start to cry will not be cut short, even to be comforted. Breakthroughs often occur when people talk through their tears and face core issues for the first time. This is illustrated by the way Anita (see previous chapter) was allowed to continue even though she was about to cry.

Group facilitators. Discussion-group leaders are members of the group, and they share their own recovery issues. They are careful not to pretend that their own problems have been solved, but instead they model gut-level honesty and caring attitudes.

Each small group of eight to fifteen needs its own facilitator. (If there are too many in a group, not everyone gets a chance to talk.) Unlike Bible-study leaders, facilitators are not the focus of attention. Some like to share first to break the ice, while others wait until the end. The facilitator may structure the meeting by giving a "time out" sign to someone who has exceeded a designated sharing time.

Having the pastor lead the group usually isn't the best choice. Few pastors can be transparent in a support group at their own churches, although ideally it shouldn't be that way. Also, pastors are considered "authorities" or "experts" (whether they like it or not), which violates the tone of fellow strugglers listening to each other. As soon as you bring in an expert of any kind to lead a group, the attitude of the members can easily change to, "I'm here; now fix me."

There may even be a few support-group members who feel resentful toward the church, and for them a pastor-leader can be irritating or threatening.

Topical sharing. Like "secretaries" in secular Twelve-Step groups, facilitators may suggest a topic for the meeting. Topics can include any of the ACDF characteristics or roles, the Twelve Steps, or even simple subjects such as loyalty, loneliness, or self-esteem. ACDFs usually like structure, and the topic helps them focus their thoughts and talk about related experiences.

Even if a topic is chosen, members may choose instead to talk about areas in which they're hurting. An insightful leader sees how the points of the various stories fit together and sums them up in a minute or two at the end.

New-member orientation. The problems of ACDFs are still fuzzy to many people, since dysfunctionality doesn't display itself in a single outward behavior such as drinking. For this reason, some groups hold an orientation session on a regular basis for newcomers. The session gives an overview of the ACDF roles, the ACDF characteristics, and the Twelve Steps as adapted for ACDFs.

Participation. Members shouldn't have to talk if they don't wish to. When people struggle to talk, trust, or feel, it's hard to open up instantly in a support group.

Some people are afraid to speak because they think their whole story will pour forth like water through a bursting dam. People who don't want to share can simply give their names and be welcomed.

Some people will talk about almost anything except their inner issues. This may help them get comfortable in the group, but it doesn't help them face their problems. Group facilitators can show the way by sharing their own feelings with "I messages," such as, "I feel anger toward my boss."

Order. People are afraid to share if they sense that someone is "fixing." If a member (usually a newcomer) says something like, "I think you ought to . . . ," the group facilitator should interrupt and repeat the "no fixing" guideline.

Facilitators may also step in when people lose their tempers. They ask angry members to step outside the group and ventilate their feelings. When they're calm, they can rejoin the group and perhaps talk about it. If this happens repeatedly, the facilitator should speak to them privately about obeying the group ground rules, and suggest that they explore this anger further with a therapist or with a friend in a one-on-one setting.

Their anger isn't wrong, but extreme rage can disrupt the group process. The group gathers to help all members, not just the extremely angry person.

Education.   Present as many different educational opportunities as possible. These help ACDFs move faster through recovery.

Having a book table at the meeting helps because it eliminates the step of going to the bookstore. If possible, include videotapes and brochures, especially Twelve-Step pamphlets, on the table. Some groups have a "freebie" pile of back issues of recovery newsletters and magazines. Members who wish to serve but don't wish to lead a group may find their niche in managing a book table.

At the meetings, announce nearby conferences or workshops. These are excellent opportunities to hear others speak who understand recovery better, and to experience a sense of community with large groups of ACDFs.

Finances. Many support groups pass a basket much like AA's seventh tradition. Other groups receive money from the church budget. Still others rely on both.

Alateen. Some parents may wish to have their children attend these secular Twelve-Step groups for teenagers and elementary children in dysfunctional families. One example of Christian teen programs is TNT ("Tried and True"). These groups for teens who have addictions or who are from dysfunctional families, were developed by Overcomers Outreach.

Ministry leaders. Most church-related ACDF groups have a ministry leader, who may or may not be the same person as the group facilitator. These leaders act as liaisons to the church and help plan and evaluate meetings. Although secular Twelve-Step groups do not have leaders, church-related groups need them as contact persons with the church staff.

Church relations. Leadership should be a mutual effort among pastoral staff, ministry leaders, group facilitators, and group members. The kind of group that seems to work best is one led by a layperson in the church, with the backing of the staff. The church provides a meeting room, permission to grow, and whatever resources it can. The ministry leader is accountable to the pastoral staff.

It's a good idea for ministry leaders to meet with pastors once a month to report the group's progress. This also keep pastors informed of potential problems so that they aren't too surprised if church members complain or if family crises develop.

Again, don't candy-coat what goes on in the group. If the meetings are sponsored by the church, the church becomes responsible for what happens there. The church could even be sued for damages (although it's not likely) if members injure themselves or others through something they claim they learned at the support group. Clear, consistent communication between leaders and the church staff can prevent these difficulties.

Problems To Expect

Sporadic attendance by those in denial. It seems to take six to nine consecutive weeks of attending a support group for a person to break out of denial. Even for those who already admit that they are ACDFs, it takes time to let their hidden pain surface. "Looking-good Christian" ACDFs have become experts at faking the "abundant life" (John 10:10, KJV) and may have an especially difficult time. When denial takes over, it's easy to skip meetings. Then the pain returns, and meetings become a priority again.

Critics. Frequently a person comes for two weeks, skips the third, and then shows up the fourth week to say, "I didn't come last week because my friend said this was a New Age group."

What do you say to critics? Some of their questions that leaders should expect to be asked are included at the end of this chapter. Support groups are so different from other groups in the church program that many people in the church will not understand them.

Sometimes we bring on criticism through our own good intentions. We have found such healing in support groups that we may exaggerate their importance as the answer to all problems. They do help some people tremendously but usually only those who have the problem and who are searching for answers.

Experience has taught us that there is, however, a type of vigorous critic for whom no answer is satisfactory.

These persons are often in denial themselves. The more that people are terrified of working through the pain of their past, the more they reject others who work through it.

Curt had the following experience with a pastor friend who illustrates this kind of critic:

> Jim would always say, "Why do you go to those ACDF meetings, Curt? Don't you know that the Bible says that you're a new creation in Christ?"
>
> Over lunches, I tried to explain the relief I felt in working through ACDF issues, but I never got anywhere. I wanted Jim to understand.
>
> After two years of this, Jim surprised me by saying that he had grown up in an alcoholic family. Then he talked nonstop for hours.
>
> "I never felt that anyone loved me," he said. "I'm working myself to death in the ministry to prove that I deserve to be loved, to prove that I'm not a failure. I guess you would call me a churchaholic. My wife is so fed up with me that she's thinking of divorcing me."
>
> I suggested to Jim that he visit our support group.
>
> "No," Jim insisted, "I can't talk about this with other people. Then they'll know that I'm not the person they think I am. The pastor has to have his life together."
>
> "But why?" I pleaded. "You can't live on a pedestal. Isn't it lonely up there?"
>
> Jim began reading about ACDF issues. He went to support groups and to therapy. He gradually opened up his life to God. After a few months, Jim realized he had been sexually abused when he was eight and that this was one of the reasons he had become so hardened. Once again, a rush of feelings overwhelmed him, but through this pain, he grew.
>
> Jim's ministry now is much deeper. He addresses people's inner issues and speaks to their hearts. The church has doubled in size, and his marriage is blossoming.

If critics like Jim are badgering you, be patient. Answer their questions, and don't expect to make much headway. When they're ready, listen.

You may be wondering . . .

Q *What if I intensely dislike someone in my support group?*
A This person probably reminds you of a parent, sibling, or friend who hurt you. Part of recovery is dealing with those people.

Listen to that person. Within the safety of the support group, you can recall your resentments toward that person, face them, and find a way to relate to that person. Jeanine found this to be true.

> Hal was disgusting to me. He was supposedly in recovery from alcoholism, but his attitudes didn't show it. He bragged about his good job. He put down his wife. He had all the traits I loathed in my alcoholic father.
>
> When Hal smiled at me, I turned away. *If he ever tries to hug me,* I thought, *I'll slug him.*
>
> Then, in a rare moment, Hal dropped his guard and shared his pain with the group. He talked about how much he loved his wife, but he had no idea how to show her.
>
> As a child Hal had been punished severely by his parents. As he described those punishments, I wept. I could remember hearing stories of how my alcoholic grandmother beat my own dad. No wonder my father couldn't show love to me.
>
> After the meeting, I thanked Hal for sharing his story, and we talked. I even explained how I had hated him, and he listened quietly. I got up to leave and then turned around to hug him.
>
> He cried, too.
>
> Knowing Hal was the key that helped me want to understand and forgive my own father.

Q *Why do people who never use foul language use it in Christian support groups?*

A Our culture links foul language with intense anger and with gut-level honesty, and people slip into it in those settings. Also, ACDFs often grew up in homes where foul language was used constantly, but as Christians they put the childhood "tapes" of that language on the back burner. As they recall their childhood, they hear that old language. When they express intense emotional hurts, it comes out.

Q *Why don't more church-related ACDF groups change the language of the Twelve Steps to reflect Jesus Christ?*

A Many leaders of Christian recovery groups agree that keeping the exact Twelve-Step wording is crucial. Many times people who have been attending secular Twelve-Step groups visit church-related groups because they have heard about the Higher Power and have become interested in God. If the Christian group that they visit uses a method radically different from the Twelve-Step method, they usually don't stay. When the traditions are similar, these people often accept Christ or renew their faith.

CHAPTER 17

Leaders Who Make the Church a Safe Place

When the Jesus People movement swept America in the 60s and 70s, the Church reacted against it. Then the Church gradually incorporated the movement's major themes so that the Church is now more warm, open, honest, and enthusiastic both in worship services and in church life.

The recovery movement will change the church with equal force. We can expect to see an even greater emphasis on trust, honesty, openness, acceptance, bonding, and the processing of feelings. Christians will refuse to accept shame and simplistic solutions to problems.

Leaders who are unfamiliar with the recovery movement may find themselves confused and even put off by people who talk about recovery. It's happening even now, but it can be avoided.

Here are some specific strategies to help church leaders handle this change. We don't offer these as a plea for leaders to pander to the newest psychological whim. Our experience with ACDF support groups has been that they bring a church closer to what it was designed to be—a place of healing and restoration.

To Get Started

Attend an ACA/ACDF support-group meeting. Listen to the struggle that is expressed, both verbal and nonverbal, at the meetings. Consider how the Twelve Steps reflect spiritual principles. (Note the corresponding Scriptures mentioned in Appendix 2.)

If you attend a secular Twelve-Step meeting, you may see some behaviors you find objectionable. Set these aside, and remember that the Twelve-Step movement is not a specifically Christian organization. It shouldn't be critiqued as such.

Investigate the dysfunctionality of your own family, and work through it. Since most families have some dysfunctionality, we're wiser to study it than to deny it. How was your family dysfunctional (see Chapters 3 and 4)? Do you often act out of one of the dysfunctional family roles (responsible child, acting-out child, adjuster, placater)? The life of a church leader can be stressful with meetings, expectations, and telephone calls. Dysfunctional family issues need to be faced.

Working through these issues prepares us to be better servants. Here's what Eric, who is a pastor, discovered:

> My ACDF recovery has been like a makeover in my attitude in the ministry. Before my recovery, I condemned myself a lot, and I saw my low self-esteem as a personal failure, not as the logical product of my background.
>
> My recovery boosted my self-confidence with others. I quit trying to "suck in" other people's approval, and I can now relate more objectively to them. I quit wondering if I was okay. Had I said anything wrong? Do these people like me? Before recovery, if someone passed me in the hall without speaking, I assumed that that person was upset with me. It didn't occur to me that he or she was concentrating on who to ask to take an absent teacher's place. Now I'm not so consumed with the other person's approval, so I'm free to tune in to that person's needs.
>
> I used to mistrust compliments because I was so insecure about my worth. I figured that any positive strokes meant that someone wanted something from me. Now, in recovery, I accept compliments at face

value, and I no longer feel the need to exaggerate my achievements so that people will like me.

My devotional time is much better, too. I don't have to prove myself to God, so I don't rigidly time my Bible-reading and prayer. I feel loved and accepted, and so I can respond to God better because I don't have a formula to follow to be an acceptable Christian.

Leaders may be too self-conscious to work through these issues in a group within their congregations but may choose to attend a support group at a different church. This is understandable, since some people relish negative details about church leaders. In some areas, pastors, priests, and leaders have started their own local groups to ensure greater confidentiality.

To Build Up Others

Help new Christians integrate their faith with their dysfunctional family issues.   What church hasn't wondered about the revolving door that brings people in the front and shuffles them out the back? Why do we keep so few new members? One possible reason is that new Christians need to get rid of their distorted views of God that come from their families of origin. In short, they need ACDF recovery. Many also struggle with compulsive behavior.

Stan was an alcoholic and an ACDF. He held down a respectable job, and no one but his family suspected his alcoholism. He never went out drinking, but he kept a refrigerator full of beer in the garage, where he worked on his model train.

Since the men at his wife's church seemed friendly, Stan started going to church with her. He liked what he heard, so he quit drinking. But the anger inside him still raged—it didn't seem as if God were helping him. People at church were polite to him, but no one, including the well-meaning pastor, ever guessed what Stan was struggling with.

Within six months, Stan stopped going to church. He felt phony trying to be calm like those people at church. He left feeling even guiltier in front of God than before.

As church leaders learn to recognize alcoholism and ACDF problems, this "revolving door" phenomenon will happen less frequently. They can suggest a Twelve-Step group or even a church-related support group if they have one. This helps new Christians to deal with the hurts of their pasts and to relate to God in healthy ways.

Start support groups for ACDFs and the addicted. Give to a program for dysfunctional-family members the same priority that you give to missions, child care, and teaching. It will positively affect all those other areas. When people share honestly in a support group, the energy multiplies, and the church catches on fire.

Recommend professionals as needed. Pastors, leaders, and therapists can work as a team to identify and help ACDFs in the church. Pastoral training doesn't often include the treatment of all the problems that ACDFs have. Sadly, the following story has occurred in some churches:

> Patty struggled with ACDF issues and with bulimia. At her church, she was prayed for repeatedly, and she attended the church's support group. Her pastor told her that therapists were a waste of time.
>
> For four years she struggled. She often became depressed and told the group, "I would kill myself if I didn't have my sons to raise."
>
> Finally, Patty became so depressed that she lost her job. She applied for government assistance, and the social worker insisted she see a psychiatrist at the county clinic. Her church friends told her not to go, but she was so desperate that she tried it.

After examining Patty, the psychiatrist explained that her years of depression had caused a severe chemical imbalance. The psychiatrist wanted to give Patty drug therapy to balance the chemicals in her body so that she could face life with the necessary physiological resources.

Patty agreed to try it even though her church friends once again advised her not to "become a drug addict." The depression lifted, and as it did, Patty returned to her support group to deal with her ACDF issues and her bulimia. Her psychiatrist gradually released her from drug therapy, and Patty was free to work through her recovery.

As church leaders understand that some people are plagued with complex physiological problems, they will understand the importance of professional help. This isn't to say that prayer doesn't work—just that God doesn't operate in a closed system in which prayer is his only tool for healing.

To Avoid Misunderstandings

Teach and lead with an awareness of ACDF tendencies. When you teach, recognize that ACDFs see God, Scripture, and the Christian life through the smoked glass of their dysfunctional upbringing, and be careful not to fuel that fire. Consider ACDF issues, especially the myths in Chapter 9, after you prepare a teaching presentation, and ask yourself how it could be misunderstood.

As you solicit workers, go out of your way to avoid appealing to codependent attitudes. Ask, "Is God moving you to do this?" —not, "The church needs you, and you're the only one who can do this." Help people to operate within their spiritual gifts and within the causes that touch their hearts.

Acknowledge the struggle of the Christian life. Much of "pop" Christianity offers "easy answers" to questions that are actually quite complex. "Just pray about it" is one of those spiritual Band-Aids. Too often, that phrase conjures up a vision of a person rattling off a one- or two-sentence prayer and the problem magically disappearing. Prayer is difficult work, and it involves constant surrender to God in every area of our lives.

Examine lessons, sermons, and over-the-back-fence counseling to see which ones acknowledge that Christians struggle. Ask yourself questions such as these:

- Do I give flip, "Christianese" answers?
- Do I show empathy for other people's pain?
- Do I balance God's demand for obedience with his love?
- Do I connect the struggling people with the helpful resource-people within our church?
- Do I pray with strugglers afterward, rather than simply offering platitudes?

Mother's Day and Father's Day sermons should give more than do's and don'ts. Pastors need to admit their own struggles as parents. One of the most powerful parts of a sermon, lesson, or piece of advice is how the person giving it failed and what he or she did to make amends.

Understand that recovery involves struggle. Many an impatient pastor, priest, or teacher has advised an ACDF, "Don't you think it's time to move on?" If you think a person is stuck in anger or blame, ask, "What is the next step you need to take? Can we pray for you about that?" This shows patience but also gives direction.

Expect people in recovery to be blunt and bold communicators. One home-fellowship–group leader reported, "I don't like it when people from our church's ACDF support group

come to our fellowship group. They dump all their bad
feelings on everybody. They talk about how they're angry
about this and that. They embarrass the rest of us—
especially the newcomers."

These situations are ideal times to model honesty and
acceptance and to pray for the recovering person. Visitors
often follow the leader's behavior. If the leader is embarrassed, the visitor will be, too. If the leader is caring yet
firm, the visitor will respect the leader's sensitivity and the
honesty of the group.

If ACDFs complain that your church is boring or stiff,
listen to them. Don't misinterpret their blunt zealousness
as dissatisfaction with you. Ask them to share their
thoughts further. How would they change the worship service? Would they like to start a support group? You don't
have to follow all their suggestions, but their input is valuable. These people have seen their relationships with God
blossom, and they're burdened to share their faith, hope,
and experiences. Don't ignore them. If they want to start
a support group and you question their ability, walk with
them through the steps of starting a support group. If you
encourage them, ACDFs in recovery can contribute to the
success and direction of your church.

Examine your church.   Is it a healthy or unhealthy family?
At a leadership meeting, review the characteristics of the
dysfunctional family, described in Chapters 3 and 4, and
apply them to your church. Are the boundaries of individ-
ual families overstepped by church leadership? Do people
trust each other? Is there consistent reinforcement? Are
feelings ever expressed, and if so, are they expressed in
appropriate ways? Is your church an open, or a closed, system? Is there room for new approaches and independent
thinkers?

As you discover the church's strong and weak points,
tell the congregation, and emphasize how the church is

healthy and how it can become even healthier. Let the entire church work together toward becoming a healthy community.

The results of the kind of leadership we've described here are exciting. Christians feel free to deal with their crises of faith. They share openly and honestly, bearing one another's burdens (Gal. 6:2). They encourage each other toward love and good works (Heb. 10:24).

The Pastor and Priest As Wounded Healers

A pastor friend recently spoke to eight hundred pastors at a theological seminary and asked them to raise their hands if their parents or grandparents were alcoholics. Seventy-five percent raised their hands. (Note that this informal survey excluded pastors from nonalcoholic dysfunctional families.)

Does it surprise you that so many pastors who are "leading us to glory" are from dysfunctional families? It makes sense when you remember that both "placaters" and "responsible children" enjoy taking care of people. It feels good to be needed. We like to hear people say, "You really helped me during my crisis." It fills those self-esteem gaps to hear compliments on sermons and lessons. It also fulfills that need to control as pastors and priests attempt to cover all the bases by getting to the hospital, social functions, and committee meetings. It fulfills empty spiritual feelings as well, since pastors are generally considered to be a little closer to God than laity. These aren't conscious needs, of course, and many individuals become pastors with the best of intentions.

Clogged filters.   Problems occur on several levels. First, the "looking-good" church leaders have to hide that deeper pain. If they aren't careful, it shows up in the form of caustic comments during the announcements on the platform on Sunday. Leaders with unresolved ACDF issues can easily become walking volcanoes, as they erupt on themselves in physical and emotional stress. At other times, they erupt on others as they build the church into a large dysfunctional family. Sometimes the King Baby parent may lord it over church members; at other times, the codependent-parent side tries to please them all.

Also, it's scary to think that preaching may be filtered through minds that are distorted with varying degrees of unrecognized ACDF characteristics. If pastors don't understand their own misconceptions about life, they don't realize how they may be slanting the truth.

That doesn't mean that ACDFs don't make good pastors and priests. If they work through ACDF issues and have time to heal, they have the extra sensitivity and understanding of a "wounded healer." Seminaries would be wise to require their students to examine their family backgrounds.

"Wounded healers" don't shame or condemn you, because they know they have sinned in similar ways. They understand your experience and don't wish it away with, "Repeat the 'Our Father' three times a day and you'll feel better." They preach, but they also listen.

Here's an example of a pastor who is now a wounded healer:

> Brian had been a pastor for twelve years and was ready to give up. He struggled with pornography daily. After he thought a church member caught him going into an adult book store, he went to see a therapist. He told the therapist that he planned to leave the ministry because he felt he was a complete failure. During the third session, he admitted that he was having an affair.
>
> As Brian and the therapist talked about his past, Brian described his workaholic father. His dad had rarely been at home, and Brian had felt emotionally estranged from him. Brian covered his face with his hands

and said, "I've preached all this hellfire and damnation because I've been so angry with my father. I've counseled people for years and have told them that all their problems came from the sin in their lives. I used to say, 'If you'll just read the Bible more and pray, you'll be healed.' I was hardest on people who struggled with sexual problems because that was my problem."

After a while in therapy and in Sexaholics Anonymous, Brian's addictions subsided. He worked on his marriage, and it was renewed. He began several support groups in his church, and revival has occurred there.

At a leadership meeting, Brian told the leaders about what had happened to him. "I was so afraid to admit it because I thought they would fire me or at least laugh at me," says Brian. "They loved me and accepted me, so I took an even bigger risk. I told the congregation my story on a Sunday evening. I was terrified, but it went well. It even became a healing service, in which hundreds of people admitted their compulsions at the altar. It was the most exciting thing I've ever seen in the ministry."

Doesn't that sound like the kind of thing that happened in the Early Church? It can happen in your church, too.

You may be wondering . . .

Q   *What do recovering ACDFs want from me as their pastor, priest, or Bible teacher?*

A   Helen's story is similar to ones that other ACDFs tell:

As I struggled with recovery, I talked with both my pastors and with two leaders at my church. I had already found a support group and a therapist, so I had professional help, but I knew that these leaders were caring people, and I wanted them to know what I was going through. I explained my problem and my recovery to them as well as I could, but I don't think they understood it.

When I saw them after that, I hoped they would ask me how I was doing, or hug me, or offer to pray with me. None of them did. I think they felt uncomfortable and didn't know what to say. I felt embarrassed, too, because I had bared my soul, but they didn't act as if it mattered.

Church leaders can do with ACDFs what they probably do so well with other people in the congregation: listen, love, and accept.

Epilogue:
There Is Hope

Recovering ACDFs are among the toughest, sanest, and psychologically strongest people the world knows. Our willingness to recognize and admit our problems shows a capacity for personal responsibility that is unusual.

Anyone who can handle what comes up at six meetings without retreating once again into denial has begun an irreversible process of recovery. Every part of life—relationships, work, health, parenting—is affected and has a better chance for success.

Although in the past we may have used self-abuse, eating, workaholism, or obsessive relationships to cope with problems, we now choose to be free. We are discovering for ourselves safe places to shed our defenses and our denial. In these support groups, we can admit to ourselves and others how angry and hurt we have always felt. We have been released to become whole.

On occasion we may reenact our old dramas and use our old defenses as if to see whether they are necessary anymore. We find that they are not. We find that we don't need to slip back into denial and compulsive behavior. We find that we are more than survivors: we are overcomers.[1]

Looking Ahead to the 1990s and Beyond

The recovery movement is one of the fastest growing elements in the Church. If church-related support groups continue to grow at the present rate, eighty percent of all churches will offer support groups in the next twenty-five years. This is good news because support groups help the Church to become a haven for those of us from dysfunctional families—a place to get better. They help the Church achieve its goal of reconciling people to God.

We can all help the Church move in this direction. We've had a glimpse of what happens in support groups and how people can grow in their faith and obedience. Even if the Church doesn't begin using support groups, the recovery movement will continue to sweep the country anyway. When people get better, they tell others about it.

The Church now stands at a crossroads. On the one hand, people are desperate to find Christ-centered support groups, and many networks are forming. On the other hand, some churches aren't listening to this need.

We as Christian ACDFs in recovery are pioneers within the Church. Will churches embrace the recovery movement, or will recovering Christians form their own churches, as the Jesus People did in the 60s and 70s?

Our pioneering efforts will be rewarded in any case. As Christians recover, the Church will be a healthier place. More people will come to Christ.

The following story will be repeated over and over:

> Mitch grew up in an alcoholic family. His father was dead drunk for every birthday party Mitch ever had. Mitch wanted to be different from his father, so he studied hard in school and got decent grades. He had an athletic build, and he lettered in three sports.
>
> Even though Mitch never drank, he became like his dad—always moody. His romantic relationships kept exploding, and his girlfriends never knew what to expect. He married early, had two children, and then divorced.
>
> Mitch turned his focus to business and built his own software company. Even there, he gathered competitive, self-centered people around him. It seemed to him as if

the nice people always quit and found "better" jobs. Their new jobs didn't pay any better, Mitch noticed, but his former employees seemed to like their new bosses better.

Mitch married again, and after a few years that relationship began to dissolve. He wanted so much for this marriage to work that he agreed to go to a marriage counselor.

The marriage counselor, Rod, was also a pastor. Mitch liked Rod a lot ("He's a go-getter too!") so Mitch visited Rod's church. He thought the church service was stuffy, but it was one thing that he and his wife could do together.

Mitch and his wife kept working to patch things up, but their marriage didn't get much better. Rod couldn't understand why Mitch couldn't control his temper, yet Rod felt he should help Mitch. They ate breakfast together sometimes.

Then Mitch's grown son visited him and told him he was going to an ACDF support group at his church. "I'm getting a lot out of it, Dad. Would you come with me sometime?" Mitch and his son had never gotten along; maybe this would help. He went to the meeting with his son.

Mitch was uncomfortable at first. He felt as if he were coming home, but it was scary. He listened to that roomful of people and discovered that they acted just like him. They felt the same craziness inside. As he read the list of ACDF characteristics after the meeting, someone offered to explain them. "Don't worry," he laughed, "I understand them all."

Mitch began attending the group regularly, and he asked Rod to go with him. Rod was skeptical, but he wanted to help Mitch. When Rod attended, he was impressed by the honesty and sincerity he saw there. He even incorporated some of their methods into the discussion group that he led at his church.

The breakfasts that Mitch and Rod had together got more interesting. Mitch asked Rod questions about God that no one had ever asked him. When Rod got carried away in talking about Scripture, Mitch would interrupt: "But what if . . . ?" Mitch's ACDF recovery was catching on, and he began telling Rod why he was so angry. He asked Rod to pray for him and help him work through his anger. Rod was impressed again; no one had ever been so honest with him before. Mitch asked Rod about the worship service. Could they sing more songs that talked about God's love?

Rod saw how Frank, one of the church leaders, had that same inner anger that Mitch had, only Frank was much more subtle. Rod had always disliked Frank because he raised so many objections at board meetings. Now he felt compassion for Frank and invited him to come to the ACDF meeting with Mitch and him.

Frank went and was quiet after the meeting. As he drove home, he kept thinking about how he tried to control people but still wanted to please them, too. With Mitch's and Frank's support, Rod started an ACDF support group at their church.

The people who attended the meeting were surprised. It was led by Mitch, the new Christian, and Frank, the long-time Christian, who were now buddies. The people saw a side of these men that touched them and made them want recovery for themselves.

This kind of chain reaction can happen, and you may be the one to start it.

Format for the New Hope Support Group

The New Hope Support Group has developed the following format. You are welcome to use it or adapt it if you wish. You may want to develop similar materials, using your own resources. New Hope meets several times a week. Each meeting lasts an hour and a half.

Part 1: Opening (twenty-five minutes)

1. The leader for that evening introduces himself or herself and welcomes the group.
2. The group repeats the Serenity Prayer:

   God, grant me the serenity to accept the things I cannot change, the courage to change the things I can, and the wisdom to know the difference.

   Living one day at a time, enjoying one moment at a time, accepting hardship as a pathway to peace; taking, as Jesus did, this sinful world as it is, not as I would have it, trusting that You will make all things right if I surrender to Your will; so that I may be reasonably happy in this life and supremely happy with You forever in the next.

   Amen.

   Reinhold Niebuhr

3. Volunteers from the group read "The Problem" and "The Solution."

The Problem

We took on the behavior patterns of the alcoholic disease and/or dysfunctional family early in childhood and carried them into adulthood. Even though we may never take a drink ourselves, we have acquired unhealthy ways of relating with others that have given us difficulty, especially in intimate relationships.

We have "stuffed" many of our feelings from our traumatic childhoods, and we have difficulty feeling or expressing our emotions, because it hurts so much. Our comfortable feelings such as joy or happiness, can be difficult to express, too. Our being out of touch with our feelings is the larger part of our denial. We learned in our dysfunctional families the three unwritten rules— *don't talk, don't trust, don't feel*—and are still unknowingly living by those rules today.

We often feel isolated and afraid of people and of authority figures. Angry people and personal criticism frighten us. Some of us take on compulsive behaviors ourselves, marry compulsive persons and try to fix them, or both. Many of us live life from the standpoint of victims, and we are attracted by weakness in our love, friendships, and career relationships.

We are terrified of abandonment and will do almost anything to hold onto a relationship rather than experience the painful feeling of abandonment. We received this from living within a dysfunctional environment, where no one was emotionally "there" for us.

This is a description, not an indictment. We have learned to survive by becoming reactors rather than actors. What we learn, we can unlearn in the solution.

The Solution

In the solution, we learn that even though our parents gave us our physical existence, we can now look to God, our Heavenly Father, as the initiator of our new lives. We look to him to lead us to a new level of experience, and to give us direction toward lives of wholeness and healing from the past. We learn that we do not have to remain prisoners of our pasts.

Recovery starts when we begin to learn about the disease. We learn that it is threefold: we didn't *cause* it, we can't *control* it, we can't *cure* it. By becoming educated about the disease, we begin a process that eventually leads us to the forgiveness of our parents and the willingness to release them to God. We learn to focus on ourselves in the here and now, and to detach from our obsession with the dysfunctional person. We learn to love ourselves and others, even though this may take the form of "tough love." We learn that real love cannot exist without the dimension of justice.

We learn to allow ourselves to feel our feelings, and then to express them. This builds self-esteem, which is the missing ingredient in our personalities, as it was never formed in childhood. We learn that, in Christ, we are okay and are not "crazy." With God's help and the Twelve Steps based on Scriptures, we can recover from our dysfunctional past, turn our lives in a new direction, and be freed from the shame that has bound us.

4. The leader gives announcements and a short testimony. The meeting is dismissed, allowing five minutes to move to small groups.

Part 2: Small Groups (sixty minutes)

The leaders of the small groups read the rules for small discussion groups.

Rules for Small Discussion Groups

1. While others are talking, please let them finish without interruption.

2. No fixing is allowed. We are to listen, to support, and to be supported by each other in the group, not to give advice. Please save any questions until after the group is dismissed.
3. Speak in the "I" form, instead of "we," "they," or "you." This helps us take responsibility for our feelings and accept them as being valid. Examples: "I believe . . . ," rather than "They say. . . ." "I felt angry that . . . ," rather than "She made me so angry. . . ."
4. Keep the sharing time to no more than five minutes, so that others in the group will be able to share.
5. Try to share from the heart as honestly as you can. You can cry, laugh, be angry in the group, without the fear of condemnation from others.
6. Do not tell others what was said or who you saw in the group meeting.

Participants choose from the following groups to attend. Completing the Newcomers series is a prerequisite to attending the other groups.

Newcomers (six weeks)
Weeks 1–3. Visitors are introduced to ACDF problems through a three-part video that New Hope has produced. It features group members, who share their experiences; Curt, who explains the dysfunctional family; and Pastor Dave Carder, who explains how God is involved in the process. Each week includes one segment of the video, and then participants divide into groups of ten and share their reactions or ask questions.

Weeks 4–6. Facilitators spend one week each in presenting the ACDF roles, the three rules (don't talk, don't trust, don't feel), and the characteristics of birth order. Once again, participants divide into groups of ten and share their reactions or questions. (Material for weeks 4–6 may be found in this book, in the books listed in Appendix 3, and in books such as *The Birth Order Book* by Kevin Leman, Old Tappan, NJ: Fleming H. Revell, 1985.)

Fifteen Characteristics (open groups—ongoing)
These groups, each consisting of about ten people, discuss the fifteen characteristics of adult children of alcoholic/dysfunctional families, using Christian Twelve-Step guidelines such as *The Twelve Steps: A Spiritual Journey.*[1] It is an "open" group, in that anyone who has attended Newcomers is invited to attend, and it does not require a commitment of consistent attendance.

Thirteen Characteristics (closed groups—thirteen weeks)
These closed discussion-groups are limited to an agreed-upon number of people who decide to commit themselves to working together for a specific period of time. Each week, these groups discuss one of the thirteen characteristics as found in Janet G. Woititz's *Adult Children of Alcoholics* (p. 4). (Woititz's list is used in this group to avoid unnecessary duplication of the open group.)

Twelve-Step Study (closed groups—sixteen weeks)
These discussion groups, which are often assigned, use *The Twelve Steps: A Spiritual Journey.*[2] These groups take sixteen weeks instead of twelve because some of the steps, especially Step 4, require more than one week. These groups also have a twenty-eight–week format for a slower study of the steps.

Managing New Hope

Facilitator Training

These eight-week sessions are held an hour before the regular meetings. Those volunteers who wish to lead small groups must currently participate in New Hope and must have participated for at least twenty weeks. They are trained to handle support-group situations, not to act as therapists or teachers. They are "fellow travelers" who continue to work on their own recovery, and who help their groups continue to be safe places.

New Hope Council

The New Hope Council consists of five volunteers who divide the responsibilities of ordering materials, organizing set-up and clean-up, organizing refreshments, assigning testimonies and greeters, handling money, and managing the book table. The members each serve for thirteen weeks. They were originally chosen by the ministry leader, but now they find their own replacements, and terms are staggered.

Resources

New Hope currently offers resources such as the New Hope Video, a facilitator training manual, "characteristics" study-guides, and a national list of Christian ACA groups. You may send requests for products or for a price list to this address:

New Hope
First Evangelical Free Church
2801 North Brea Blvd.
Fullerton, CA 92635–2799

The Twelve Steps and the Twelve Traditions

When members of Twelve-Step groups talk about "working a program," they refer to putting the Twelve Steps of AA into action. These same Twelve Steps have been used in the ACA and ACDF movements and have helped millions. Listed below are the Twelve Steps of Alcoholics Anonymous, reworded for the ACDF by the New Hope group. See for yourself the spiritual depth of each one.

STEP ONE. We admitted we were powerless over our separation from God—that our lives had become unmanageable. (The original AA wording says, "powerless over alcohol.")

Scripture: "I know that nothing good lives in me, that is, in my sinful nature. For I have the desire to do what is good, but I cannot carry it out" (Rom. 7:18).

This idea of powerlessness is tough for ACDFs because we have believed that we were in charge of ourselves. We have worked hard to control ourselves and our environment. We have adopted the "rugged individualism" and success ethic of our culture, which says that if we just try hard enough, we'll overcome.

This first step goes against all that. It requires humility as we recognize that we are wrestling with something bigger than ourselves.

STEP TWO. We came to believe that a power greater than ourselves could restore us to sanity.

Scripture: ". . . For it is God who works in you to will and to act according to his good purpose" (Phil. 2:13).

This step opens up the idea that a solution is possible. Our "craziness" and the ways we overreact and overachieve can be changed by God, the power greater than ourselves.

STEP THREE. We made a decision to turn our will and our lives over to the care of God as we understood Him.

Scripture: "Therefore, I urge you, brothers, in view of God's mercy, to offer your bodies as living sacrifices, holy and pleasing to God—which is your spiritual worship" (Rom. 12:1).

In this step, we surrender ourselves to God. These first three steps are often abbreviated like this: (1) I can't, (2) God can, (3) so I'll let him.

STEP FOUR. We made a searching and fearless moral inventory of ourselves.

Scripture: "Let us examine our ways and test them, and let us return to the LORD" (Lam. 3:40).

In a Twelve-Step inventory, participants comb through their lives, looking for character defects in themselves but not in others.

STEP FIVE. We admitted to God, to ourselves, and to another human being the exact nature of our wrongs.

Scripture: "Therefore, confess your sins to each other and pray for each other so that you may be healed" (James 5:16a).

The nearly lost art of biblical confession to God and to others helps us know and say the truth about ourselves.

STEP SIX. We were entirely ready to have God remove all these defects of character.

Scripture: "Humble yourselves before the Lord, and he will lift you up" (James 4:10).

It's one thing to recognize our character defects but quite another to be willing to change. We get comfortable in our old ways of relating to people, and change can be painful. This step says that we are ready to change.

STEP SEVEN. We humbly asked Him to remove our shortcomings.

Scripture: "If we confess our sins, He is faithful and just and will forgive us our sins and purify us from all unrighteousness" (1 John 1:9).

We become so willing to change that we ask God's help in doing so.

STEP EIGHT. We made a list of all persons we had harmed and became willing to make amends to them all.

Scripture: "Do to others as you would have them do to you" (Luke 6:31).

We take personal responsibility for our actions. We no longer bury anger. We know where it comes from, we work on those issues, and we own up to our mistakes.

STEP NINE. We made direct amends to such people wherever possible, except when to do so would injure them or others.

Scripture: "Therefore, if you are offering your gift at the altar and there remember that your brother has something against you, leave your gift there in front of the altar. First go and be reconciled to your brother; then come and offer your gift" (Matt. 5:23, 24).

We don't let our dysfunctionality excuse us, but we restore ourselves to those we have injured as a result.

STEP TEN. We continued to take personal inventory and when we were wrong promptly admitted it.

Scripture: "So, if you think you are standing firm, be careful that you don't fall!" (1 Cor. 10:12).

This self-examination is a lifelong process. We understand that we are always susceptible to sin and its effects on us.

STEP ELEVEN. We sought through prayer and meditation to improve our conscious contact with God as we understood Him, praying only for knowledge of His will for us and the power to carry that out.

Scripture: "Let the word of Christ dwell in you richly . . ." (Col. 3:16).

It isn't enough to say we are Christians or to attend church. Our faith includes personal contact with God, as well as shedding our distorted views of him and meditating on correct ones.

STEP TWELVE. Having had a spiritual awakening as a result of these steps, we tried to carry this message to others, and to practice these principles in all our affairs.

Scripture: "Brothers, if someone is caught in a sin, you who are spiritual should restore him gently. But watch yourself, or you also may be tempted" (Gal. 6:1).

We help ACDFs who are not in recovery by sharing our own stories, not by confronting them. When they ask for help, we listen and cry with them.

Sometimes it's difficult to do this because we feel safer with recovering ACDFs. We may not want to venture out into our church's overall program or into work-related activities, but doing so is part of doing the twelfth Step. We will no doubt find other ACDFs and will share our faith, hope, and experiences with them, even when it's a little scary to do so.

The Twelve Steps help ACDFs learn constructive ways to identify and manage pain. These steps propel us through our recovery and don't allow us to get stuck in anger or introspection. They bring "closure" in our recovery because they help us grow beyond our pain.

The Twelve Traditions

Here are the Twelve Traditions that AA and other Twelve-Step groups have used to help people stay focused on their recovery. We reprint them with two purposes:

1. Some of these Traditions transfer directly to a church-related support group. (Some do not, because of the church's requirement for leadership.)
2. Anyone who isn't familiar with these Traditions can read them to see the spirit in which AA developed, why it isn't a distinctly Christian organization, and why it has been so successful in alcohol recovery.

One—Our common welfare should come first: personal recovery depends upon A.A. unity.

Two—For our group purpose there is but one ultimate authority—a loving God as He may express Himself in our group conscience. Our leaders are but trusted servants; they do not govern.

Three—The only requirement for A.A. membership is a desire to stop drinking.

Four—Each group should be autonomous except in matters affecting other groups or A.A. as a whole.

Five—Each group has but one primary purpose—to carry its message to the alcoholic who still suffers.

Six—An A.A. group ought never to endorse, finance or lend the A.A. name to any related facility or outside enterprise, lest problems of money, property and prestige divert us from our primary purpose.

Seven—Every A.A. group ought to be fully self-supporting, declining outside contributions.

Eight—Alcoholics Anonymous should remain forever nonprofessional, but our service centers may employ special workers.

Nine—A.A., as such, ought never be organized; but we may create service boards or committees directly responsible to those they serve.

Ten—Alcoholics Anonymous has no opinion on outside issues; hence the A.A. name ought never be drawn into public controversy.

Eleven—Our public relations policy is based on attraction rather than promotion; we need always maintain personal anonymity at the level of press, radio and films.

Twelve—Anonymity is the spiritual foundation of all our Traditions, ever reminding us to place principles before personalities.[1]

Because church-related support groups do not follow all of these Twelve Traditions, they are not Twelve-Step groups in the purest sense of the AA tradition. True Twelve-Step groups have no leaders. A group may meet in a church building, but it is never affiliated with any church.

1. We admitted we were powerless over alcohol—that our lives had become unmanageable. 2. Came to believe that power greater than ourselves could restore us to sanity. 3. Made a decision to turn our will and our lives over to the care of God as we understood Him. 4. Made a searching and fearless moral inventory of ourselves. 5. Admitted to God, to ourselves, and to another human being the exact nature of our wrongs. 6. Were entirely ready to have God remove all these defects of character. 7. Humbly asked Him to remove our shortcomings. 8. Made a list of all persons we had harmed and became willing to make amends to them all. 9. Made direct amends to such people wherever possible, except when to do so would injure them or

others.   10. Continued to take personal inventory and when we were wrong promptly admitted it.   11. Sought through prayer and meditation to improve our conscious contact with God, as we understood Him, praying only for knowledge of His will for us and power to carry that out.   12. Having had a spiritual awakening as a result of these steps, we tried to carry this message to others, and to practice these principles in all our affairs.

The Twelve Steps are reprinted and adapted with permission of Alcoholics Anonymous World Services, Inc. Permission to reprint and adapt the Twelve Steps does not mean that AA has reviewed or approved the content of this publication, nor that AA agrees with the views expressed herein. AA is a program of recovery from alcoholism. The use of the Twelve Steps in connection with programs and activities that are patterned after AA but that address other problems does not imply otherwise.

Support-Group Resources

These are some of the many support group resources that now exist. Some churches offer their own support groups, but many still do not. You may want to consult some of these organizations, although we do not necessarily endorse any of them.

Christian Networks and Centers

Alcoholics for Christ, Inc.
1316 North Campbell Road
Royal Oak, MI 48067

Alcoholics Victorious National
   Headquarters
9370 S.W. Greenburg Rd.,
   Suite 411
Tigard, CA 97323

Christian Alcoholics Rehabili-
   tation Association
FOA Road
Pocahontas, MS 39072

Focus on the Family
Pomona, CA 91799

Liontamers
2801 North Brea Blvd.
Fullerton, CA 92635–2799

Lost and Found Inc.
9189 So. Turkey Creek Road
Morrison, CO 80465

National Association for
   Christian Recovery
P.O. Box 11095
Whittier, CA 90603

New Life Treatment Centers
P.O. Box 38
Woodstock, MN 56186

Overcomers Outreach, Inc.
2290 West Whittier Blvd.
La Habra, CA 90631

Sinners Anonymous Service
   Center
P.O. Box 26001
Austin, TX 78755–0001

Substance Abusers Victorious
One Cascade Plaza
Akron, OH 44308

If you know of other recovery networks or meetings, please add them to the national list for networking purposes. Send this information to:

New Hope
First Evangelical Free Church
2801 North Brea Blvd.
Fullerton, CA 92635-2799

Secular Groups

Adult Children of Alcoholics
Central Service Board
P.O. Box 3216
Torrance, CA 90505

The Adult Children's Center
112 East Chapman Ave.,
Suite A
Orange, CA 92666

Al-Anon/Alateen
Family Group Headquarters,
Inc.
P.O. Box 862
Midtown Station
New York, NY 10018

Alcoholics Anonymous
World Services, Inc.
468 Park Avenue South
New York, NY 10016

Children of Alcoholics
Foundation
200 Park Ave.
New York, NY 10166

Co-Dependents Anonymous
(CODA)
P.O. Box 33577
Phoenix, AZ 85067–3577

Debtors Anonymous
P.O. Box 20322
New York, NY 10025–9992

Emotions Anonymous
P.O. Box 4245
St. Paul, MN 55104

Gamblers Anonymous
P.O. Box 17173
Los Angeles, CA 90017

Narcotics Anonymous World
Service Office
16155 Wyandotte Street
Van Nuys, CA 91406

National Association for
Children of Alcoholics
31706 Coast Highway,
Suite 201
South Laguna, CA 92677

Overeaters Anonymous World
Service Office
4025 Spencer St., Suite 203
Torrance, CA 90503
P.O. Box 92870
Los Angeles, CA 90009

Secular Organizations for
  Sobriety (SOS)
P. O. Box 15781
No. Hollywood, CA 91615

Sexaholics Anonymous
P.O. Box 300
Simi Valley, CA 93062

Workaholics Anonymous
Westchester Community
  College
AAB
75 Grasslands Road
Valhalla, NY 10595

PRINT RESOURCES

There are many more books than these, but here are
some to whet your appetite. Some are written specifically
for Christians, others are not. If you don't see what you
need, check your local bookstore.

Adult Children of Dysfunctional Families

Black, Claudia. *It Will Never Happen to Me: Children of Alcoholics as Youngsters*. Denver, CO: M.A.C. Printing and Publications Division, 1982.

Bradshaw, John. *Bradshaw On: The Family*. Deerfield Beach, FL: Health Communications, 1988.

Bradshaw, John. *Bradshaw On: Healing the Shame that Binds You*. Deerfield Beach, FL: Health Communications, 1988.

Bradshaw, John. *Homecoming: Reclaiming and Championing Your Inner Child*. New York: Bantam Books, 1990.

Christians in Recovery. *The Twelve Steps for Christians*. San Diego, CA: Recovery Publications, 1988.

Christians in Recovery. *The Twelve Steps: A Spiritual Journey*. San Diego, CA: Recovery Publications, 1988.

Friel, John, and Friel, Linda. *Adult Children*. Deerfield Beach, FL: Health Communications, 1988.

Satir, Virginia. *Peoplemaking*. Palo Alto, CA: Science and Behavior Books, 1972.

Wegscheider-Cruse, Sharon. *Another Chance: Hope and Health for the Alcoholic Family.* Palo Alto, CA: Science and Behavior Books, Inc., 1989.

Woititz, Janet. *Adult Children of Alcoholics.* Deerfield Beach, FL: Health Communications, 1983.

Woititz, Janet. *The Struggle for Intimacy.* Deerfield Beach, FL: Health Communications, 1985.

Wright, H. Norman. *Always Daddy's Girl.* Ventura, CA: Regal Books, 1990.

Spiritual Growth in Dysfunctionality

Johnson, Jan. *When It Hurts to Grow.* Wheaton, IL: Victor Books, 1991.

Seamands, David. *Healing for Damaged Emotions.* Wheaton, IL: Victor Books, 1989.

Seamands, David. *Healing of Memories.* Wheaton, IL: Victor Books, 1985.

Addictions

Alcoholics Anonymous. *Alcoholics Anonymous, The Big Book.* New York: Alcoholics Anonymous World Services, 1976.

Alcoholics Anonyous. *Twelve Steps and Twelve Traditions.* New York: Alcoholics Anonymous World Services, 1952.

Bill B. *The Compulsive Overeater.* Minneapolis, MN: CompCare Publications, 1981.

Carnes, Patrick, Ph.D. *Out of the Shadows: Understanding Sexual Addiction.* Minneapolis, MN: CompCare Publications, 1983.

LeSourd, Sandra Simpson. *The Compulsive Woman.* Old Tappan, NJ: Fleming H. Revell, 1987.

Miller, Keith. *Hope in the Fast Lane.* San Francisco: Harper & Row, 1987.

Abuse

Allender, Dan. *The Wounded Heart: Hope for Adult Victims of Childhood Sexual Abuse*. Colorado Springs: NavPress, 1990.

Brewer, Connie, ed. *Escaping the Shadows Seeking the Light: Christians in Recovery from Childhood Sexual Abuse*. San Francisco: HarperCollins, 1991.

Finley, Midge, and Joann Felmuth. *We Weep for Ourselves and Our Children*. San Francisco: HarperCollins, 1990.

Frank, Jan. *A Door of Hope*. San Bernardino, CA: Here's Life Publishers, 1987.

Notes

Chapter 1. "Saved," But Still Sick

1. John Friel and Linda Friel, *Adult Children: The Secrets of Dysfunctional Families* (Deerfield Beach, FL: Health Communications, 1988), 17.

2. Virginia Satir, *Peoplemaking* (Palo Alto, CA: Science and Behavior Books, 1972), 18.

Chapter 2. Dysfunctionality: The Handicap of Being Human

1. "Don't talk, don't trust, don't feel" are three rules that Claudia Black popularized in her book *It Will Never Happen to Me* (Denver, CO: M.A.C. Printing and Publications Division, 1982), chap. 3, 31–52.

2. David Seamands, *Healing for Damaged Emotions* (Wheaton, IL: Victor Books, 1989), 69.

Chapter 3. What It Was Like To Be a Child in a Dysfunctional Family (Part 1)

1. "Children of Alcoholics Battle Trauma as Adults," *Los Angeles Times*, 24 September 1985, sec. V.

2. "National Association for Children of Alcoholics," National Association for Children of Alcoholics (South Laguna, CA: NACoA).

3. "Gene Associated with Alcoholism Identified," *UCLA News*, 17 April 1990.

4. "National Association for Children of Alcoholics."

Chapter 4. What It Was Like To Be a Child in a Dysfunctional Family (Part 2)

1. L. C. Ellwood, "Effects of Alcoholism As a Family Illness on Child Behavior and Development," *Military Medicine* 145, no. 3 (1980): 188–92, D. Miller and M. Jang, "Children of Alcohol-

ics: A Twenty-Year Longitudinal Study," *Social Work Research and Abstracts* 13 (1977): 23–29. In Deborah Helen Krois, "Children of Alcoholics" (Ph.D. diss., Biola University 1987), 19.

2. M. L. Kammeier, "Adolescents From Families With and Without Alcohol Problems," *Quarterly Journal of Studies on Alcohol* 32 (1971): 364–72, in Krois, 14–15.

3. I. Nylander, "Children of Alcoholic Fathers," *Acta Paediatrica* 49, no. 1 (1960): 1–134, in Krois, 16.

4. J. R. Morrison and M. A. Steward, "A Family Study of the Hyperactive Syndrome," *Biological Psychiatry* 3 (1971): 189–95, and D. P. Cantwell, "Psychiatric Illness in the Families of Hyperactive Children," *Archives of General Psychiatry* 27 (1972): 414–17, in Krois, 20.

5. E. W. Fine, L. W. Yudin, J. Holmes, and S. Heinemann, "Behavioral Disorders in Children With Parental Alcoholism," *Annals of the New York Academy of Sciences* 23 (1976): 507–17, in Krois, 21–22.

6. J. F. McLachlan, R. L. Walderman, and S. Thoman, "A Study of Teenagers With Alcoholic Parents," *Donwood Institute Research Monograph* 3 (1973); P. A. O'Gorman, "Self-Concept, Locus on Control, and Perception of Father in Adolescents From Homes With and Without Severe Drinking Problems" (Ph.D. diss., Fordham University, 1975); J. Hughes, "Adolescent Children of Alcoholic Parents and the Relationship of Alateen to These Children," *Journal of Consulting and Clinical Psychology* 45, no. 5 (1977): 946–47; and D. W. Goodwin, F. Schulsinger, L. Hermansen, and S. B. Guze, "Psychopathology in Adopted and Nonadopted Daughters of Alcoholics," *Archives of General Psychiatry* 34 (1977): 1005–9, in Krois, 24.

7. Hughes, 946–47; Miller and Jang, 23–29; M. E. Chafetz, H. T. Blane, and M. J. Hill, "Children of Alcoholics: Observations in a Child Guidance Clinic," *Quarterly Journal of Studies on Alcohol* 31 (1971): 687–98, in Krois, 27.

8. "Why Stress Makes You Stupid," *M Magazine* (May 1988): 72.

9. Erik Erikson, *Childhood and Society* (New York: W.W. Norton, 1963), 247–73.

Chapter 5. Roles That Get Us through Childhood

1. These roles were noted and named by Claudia Black in her book *It Will Never Happen to Me,* and are used widely in the ACDF movement. Sharon Wegscheider-Cruse in *Another Chance: Hope and Health for the Alcoholic Family* uses other names for similar roles, which we have also included.

Chapter 6. My Past Lives in Me

1. Hugh Missildine, M.D., *Your Inner Child of the Past* (New York: Simon & Schuster, 1963), 1–50.

2. This concept was also developed by Missildine in "It Takes Four to Make a Marriage," *Your Inner Child of the Past,* 56–63.

3. Krois, 32.

Chapter 7. Scrambling To Be Adults

1. Janet Geringer Woititz originated these specific characteristics in her book *The Struggle for Intimacy* (Deerfield Beach, FL: Health Communications, 1985), 85–98. We have placed them in a different order and have provided our own comments.

2. Woititz and others say, "We guess at what normal is." We have changed this because we believe that some degree of dysfunctionality is so common that it might be termed "normal." Dysfunctional people do feel as if they are guessing at what healthy behavior is.

3. Woititz lists another characteristic: "ACAs are either super responsible or super irresponsible" (p. 97).

Chapter 8. Blurred Spiritual Vision

1. Seamands, *Healing of Memories* (Wheaton, IL: Victor Books, 1985), 98–99.

2. Lawrence O. Richards, *The Teacher's Commentary* (Wheaton, IL: Victor Books, 1988), 729.

Chapter 10. "Compulsive? Who Me?"

1. D. W. Goodwin, F. Schulsinger, L. Hermansen, S. B Guze, and G. Winokur, (1973), *Archives of General Psychiatry* 28, 238–43, in Krois, (1987), 13–14.

2. Patrick Carnes, *Out of the Shadows* (Minneapolis: CompCare Publications, 1983), 26–47.

Chapter 11. How Soon Will This Be Over?

1. This is an informal observation of physician Dr. Willard Hawkins from his private medical practice with Harbor Family Practice in Fullerton, CA.

Chapter 12. Reparenting the Child Within

1. "Charter Statement," National Association for Children of Alcoholics (South Laguna, CA: NACoA).

Chapter 15. Support Groups: Bearing Each Other's Burdens

1. We are indebted to psychologist Dr. Earl Henslin for his study of the AA movement and for these observations.

2. Facts taken from "Foreword to Second Edition," *Alcoholics Anonymous* (New York: Alcoholics Anonymous World Services, 1976), xv–xxi.

3. Charles Leershen et al., "Unite and Conquer," *Newsweek,* 5 February 1990, 55.

4. "We Agnostics" in *Alcoholics Anonymous,* 45.

5. "We Agnostics," 44.

6. "Foreword to Second Edition" in *Alcoholics Anonymous,* xx.

7. "Foreword to Second Edition," xvii–xviii.

Epilogue: There Is Hope

1. The first four paragraphs of the Epilogue are adapted from The New Hope Packet, p. 4, reprinted with permission by First Evangelical Free Church, Fullerton, CA.

Appendix 1: Format for the New Hope Support Group

1. *The Twelve Steps: A Spiritual Journey* (San Diego, CA: Recovery Publications, 1988), 1–4.

2. *The Twelve Steps,* 5–147.

Appendix 2: The Twelve Steps and the Twelve Traditions

1. *Alcoholics Anonymous,* 564.